CREATIVE

BIBLE LESSONS IN

Youth Specialties Titles

Professional Resources

Developing Spiritual Growth in Junior High Students
Developing Student Leaders
Equipped to Serve
Help! I'm a Sunday School Teacher!
Help! I'm a Volunteer Youth Worker!
How to Recruit and Train Volunteer Youth Workers
The Ministry of Nurture
One Kid at a Time
Peer Counseling in Youth Groups
Advanced Peer Counseling in Youth Groups

Discussion Starter Resources

Get 'Em Talking
High School TalkSheets
Junior High TalkSheets
High School TalkSheets: Psalms and Proverbs
Junior High TalkSheets: Psalms and Proverbs
More High School TalkSheets
More Junior High TalkSheets
Parent Ministry TalkSheets
Would You Rather . . . ?

Ideas Library

Ideas Combo 1–4, 5–8, 9–12, 13–16, 17–20, 21–24, 25–28, 29–32, 33–36, 37–40, 41–44, 45–48, 49–52, 53, 54, 55
Ideas Index

Youth Ministry Programming

Compassionate Kids
Creative Bible Lessons on the Life of Christ
Creative Programming Ideas for Junior High Ministry
Creative Socials and Special Events
Dramatic Pauses
Facing Your Future
Great Fundraising Ideas for Youth Groups
Great Retreats for Youth Groups
Greatest Skits on Earth
Greatest Skits on Earth, Volume 2
Hot Illustrations for Youth Talks
Hot Talks
Junior High Game Nights
More Junior High Game Nights
Play It! Great Games for Groups
Play It Again! More Great Games for Groups
Road Trip
Super Sketches for Youth Ministry
Teaching the Bible Creatively
Up Close and Personal: How to Build Community in Your Youth Group

Clip Art

ArtSource Volume 1—Fantastic Activities
ArtSource Volume 2—Borders, Symbols, Holidays, and Attention Getters
ArtSource Volume 3—Sports
ArtSource Volume 4—Phrases and Verses
ArtSource Volume 5—Amazing Oddities and Apalling Images
ArtSource Volume 6—Spiritual Topics
ArtSource Volume 7—Variety Pack

Video

Edge TV
God Views
The Heart of Youth Ministry: A Morning with Mike Yaconelli
Next Time I Fall in Love Video Curriculum
Promo Spots for Junior High Game Nights
Understanding Your Teenager Video Curriculum
Witnesses

Student Books

Grow for It Journal
Grow for It Journal Through the Scriptures
Next Time I Fall in Love
Wild Truth Journal
101 Things to Do During a Dull Sermon

CREATIVE
BIBLE LESSONS IN

Encounters with Jesus

Janice and Jay Ashcraft

ZondervanPublishingHouse

A Division of HarperCollinsPublishers

Creative Bible Lessons in John: Encounters with Jesus

Copyright © 1995 by Youth Specialties, Inc.

Youth Specialties Books, 1224 Greenfield Drive, El Cajon, California 92021, are published by Zondervan Publishing House, 5300 Patterson, S.E., Grand Rapids, Michigan 49530.

Ashcraft, Janice and Jay.
Creative Bible lessons in John : encounters with Jesus / Janice and Jay Ashcraft
     p. cm.
  ISBN 0–310–20769–X
  1. Bible N.T. John—Commentaries. 2. Bible—Study and teaching (Secondary)—Activity programs. 3. Activity programs in Christian education. I. Title.
BS2616.A74 1995
226.5'0071'2–dc20
                                                    95-34989
                                                      CIP

Unless otherwise noted, all Scripture references are taken from the Holy Bible: New International Version (North American Edition), copyright © 1973, 1978, 1984 by the International Bible Society. Used by permission of Zondervan Bible Publishers.

Edited by Noel Becchetti and Lorraine Triggs
Typography and Design by Jack Rogers

Printed in the United States of America

95 96 97 98 99/ /5 4 3 2 1

Dedication

This book is dedicated to my children Haley, Jesse, and Zoe. Watching them grow up has taught me more than they will ever know.

Special thanks

My wife, Janice, is responsible for getting this project off the ground. She transformed many of my jumbled ideas into intelligible information. She was great at finding new ways to approach these lessons when I ran into roadblocks. Many of the ideas in this book were field tested with the students at First Baptist Church in Narragansett, Rhode Island. I have appreciated their valuable feedback. Cheryl Blumenbaum, Ruth Busby, Rebecca Erickson, Jeff Balch, Karen Smith, Rob Allen, and Cindi Storti have all been an encouragment to me as they have served God by ministering to young people. My sister Rene provided some much–needed computer expertise. My thanks also goes to Doug Fields who paved the way for this book by providing a pattern to follow. Finally, this book would not have been possible without Noel Becchetti who guided me through the entire writing process.

Table of Contents

Introduction

Everyone loves a story! That is probably the reason John filled his gospel with stories about people. Time after time John tells about people who met with Jesus at critical points in each of their lives. The lessons in this book are designed to help your students identify with these people who encountered Christ. The gospel of John is loaded with deep theological truth. The lessons in this book will help your students realize that truth about God can be very practical. John tells about real people with real problems. Your students will learn that an encounter with Jesus can be just as relevant for them as it was for the people who walked the dusty roads of a tiny, middle eastern country nearly 2,000 years ago. Look over the first three chapters before you jump into the studies. If you're a veteran, they'll be reminders; if you're new to youth ministry, they'll give you a foundation to be a more effective teacher. As we dust off some all-too-familiar stories, we hope this book will bring the gospel of John to life for your students. More importantly, we hope this book will serve as a tool to help your students encounter Jesus, face to face. May God use you as you continue to serve him.

Janice and Jay Ashcraft

Chapter One
Why Use Creativity in Your Teaching?

I can't recall any students in my years of youth ministry who have come running to youth group screaming, "Give me another Bible talk, I can't get enough of them." Most students manage to sit still through youth talks week after week (key word: "most") only because they know there's a lot more to youth group than just the talk.

When the talk is packaged creatively, however, students are usually much more interested in learning God's truth (key word: "usually"). Using a creative approach isn't the cure-all to energizing the apathetic or uninterested student, but it does help. Not only does creative teaching capture your students' attention, it also communicates to them that you're willing to do whatever it takes to get the message across. They see you adapting your teaching style in order to enlighten them with God's timeless truths.

There are three reasons why I get excited about creative teaching:

Creative teaching makes Sunday school and youth group exciting.
The word *boring* has been defined as doing the same thing over and over again. And it has been said that *insanity* is doing the same thing over and over again while expecting different results. If both of these are true, many youth groups are boring and their leaders are insane. Teaching the same way over and over gets boring . . . no matter how good a communicator we may be.

Our Sunday school programs and youth groups should shatter the stereotype that church is boring. I'm not suggesting we turn our youth ministries into circuses so they're not dull, but I am suggesting we think through what we do and why we teach the way we do.

If anyone had the right to simply lecture and expect his students to listen it would be Jesus. Yet Jesus refused to rely solely on lectures. John tells how Jesus did things—like turning over the money changers' tables in the temple, feeding a famished crowd, washing his disciples' dirty feet, and smearing mud across the eyes of a man who could not see. John's gospel describes Jesus using a wide variety of creative teaching methods to capture the interest and imagination of his listeners. We would do well to follow *his* example.

When time is invested in creativity, it makes youth group a different place. Sunday school gets exciting; youth meetings become fun. The truths within God's Word are exciting—let's make our teaching methods equally exciting.

Students learn in different ways.

I learn best by seeing and hearing. My wife learns best by experiencing. Our son learns best by observing. Our oldest daughter learns best by reading and listening. Our youngest daughter takes information any way she can get it. We are all in the same family, yet we all have different learning styles.

If we always teach the same way, we'll reach only a fraction of our students. Unfortunately, chances are high that the small group we reach only learn "pieces" from our styles, because they probably have additional learning styles that complement their dominant styles.

If students learn in different ways, we would be wise to teach with different methods if we're going to minister effectively.

Students actually look forward to learning.

Imagine having students who look forward to learning God's Word. It's possible, and even probable as we develop creative teaching methods and make ourselves open to new approaches.

It is doubtful that the story of the building of the tabernacle in the book of Exodus would make the top ten list of best–loved Bible stories, yet that particular lesson stands out in my wife's mind. She was deeply impressed with the glorious symbolism and foreshadowing of Christ and the church. She was in junior high when her Sunday school teacher taught on that subject.

So how did this teacher cause a group of rowdy junior highers to get excited about a subject most of us would be yawning through? Not by lecturing. Not by reading from a teachers' manual. Instead she encouraged her students to get involved with the lesson. She invited them to her home where they planned and built a small scale model of the tabernacle. She then had them present their work before the congregation during a special service. Now that kind of creative Bible lesson makes a lasting impression.

It's an awesome responsibility and privilege to teach God's Word. The message is lifechanging! The methods of communicating are open for development and experimentation. My prayer is that you will be open for a little variation. The results will be worth your effort . . . and some students eventually will thank you for it (key words: "some" and "eventually").

Chapter Two
Ten Components of Effective Teaching

My intention for this chapter isn't to provide you with a doctoral thesis on methods of biblical instruction. There are several outstanding books available on teaching methods. In this chapter I want to highlight ten ways students learn. I'm sure there are more, but these are the ten I keep in front of me as I prepare a lesson. I use this list as a reminder of how students learn and as a challenge for me to use a different method than I used before.

Doing

When you are able to get your students to do something with your message, you have succeeded! Participation shoots a students' learning curve straight up.

I could teach on servanthood for six years, and my students could have all the head knowledge needed to articulate a theology of service and proudly quote a few Scriptures, but it doesn't mean they'll be servants. When I provide an opportunity for my students to serve a widow in our church, they learn more about servanthood through this one act than through hours of listening to me talk.

The Christian faith can be experienced, and your students will become more mature when you give them opportunities to experience and practice God's truth.

Seeing

Many of your students were weaned on *Sesame Street* and MTV and are accustomed to learning through observation. They watch loads of TV and are primed to learn through this medium. When you can make your message one they can see, you create a visual memory that will last for a significant length of time.

Acting

Many students love the opportunity to read Scripture and act out their interpretations. Acting gets your students up, moving, involved, interacting, and thinking of how God's Word might be translated in today's vernacular. This medium helps cement passages into your students' memories.

Writing

Creative writing or the expression of feelings on paper is an effective way for adolescents to communicate and learn. Many students dabble with poetry or songwriting; they can apply these methods to exploring biblical truths when given the opportunity.

Creating

If you encourage your students to channel their creative juices in the direction of God's Word, you may find that it is more difficult to slow them down than to get them started. Each summer I encourage my students to be creative in the way they report back to the church about their summer missions trips. I have never ceased to be amazed at the variety of methods they find to communicate their experiences.

Playing

By the time my oldest daughter was a year old, she had developed a very definite food preference. She preferred *not* to eat vegetables. While my daughter did not like vegetables, she did love cheese. My wife and I started putting cheese on every vegetable dish we made. Our daughter became so busy enjoying the melted cheese she hardly even noticed that she was eating all those healthy vegetables.

Some of our kids are conditioned to resist learning in the same way my daughter resisted eating what was good for her. It is always good to have a little "melted cheese" to help whet the appetites of your students. Playing games is one of the best ways I know to encourage your kids to learn. The wonderful thing about play is that it is designed to be fun. When kids are playing games, they are usually having so much fun they don't seem to mind learning. Sometimes they don't even notice.

Hearing

Few students learn best by listening to a teacher. They still may learn, but lecturing is one of the least effective forms of communication.

What increases the effectiveness of teaching through speaking is when stories are used. As you know, storytelling was a favorite method used by Jesus, and it was very effective. Though students won't admit it, I'm convinced they still love stories. Your teenagers have heard hundreds of stories during their childhood; if given a choice between listening to a talk or hearing a good story, I'm sure they'll choose the story every time.

Drawing

Some of the most creative and artistic students in your youth group are the last people who will volunteer to act out or publicly share their feelings. Many artistic students are reserved and choose to express themselves through their art. Give them an opportunity to share their faith by drawing what they "see" from Scripture. Give them a passage and allow them to interpret it through their drawing. You'll see some interesting results, and you'll minister to students who are hard to reach through traditional methods.

Cooperating

Some of your students may learn best by working with other students. I know some highly relational students who can't do anything alone, but when given the opportunity to work with others, they discover a new depth of understanding.

Living

This last component is directed to you as the teacher. Your students are learning much from you and how you live your life. They are absorbing messages about God's love and the Christian faith each time they interact with you or watch you in action. Don't underestimate the power of your lifestyle.

I really don't remember very many messages I heard as a teenager, but the truths I observed in my leaders made a lasting impression. Adolescents are quick to sniff out phonies. They are looking for real people to be real models of what it means to love God and live as a Christian. Maybe that's why James wrote in his letter, "Not many of you should presume to be teachers, my brothers, because you know that we who teach will be judged more strictly" (James 3:1).

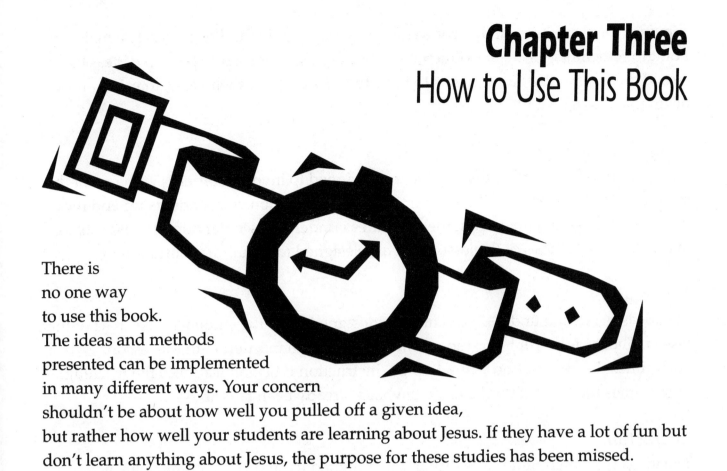

Chapter Three
How to Use This Book

There is
no one way
to use this book.
The ideas and methods
presented can be implemented
in many different ways. Your concern
shouldn't be about how well you pulled off a given idea,
but rather how well your students are learning about Jesus. If they have a lot of fun but
don't learn anything about Jesus, the purpose for these studies has been missed.

I know youth ministry, and I know how to communicate to the students in my youth
group—but I don't know how to communicate to your students. No one knows your
group better than you. The ideas presented throughout this book will work in general,
but feel free to tweak these ideas to work for you specifically. The ideas in this book are
not infallible. If one doesn't work for you, get rid of it or use it as a springboard for
another idea that will work with your students.

Let me go over a few steps on how you can use these creative Bible lessons effectively.

Familiarize yourself with the lesson format

To bring some continuity to the twelve lessons in this book, I've chosen to use, in
varying order and combinations, these five components:

Introduction

The ideas presented under this section are designed to hook students' interest in a
light, fun, and upbeat manner. Some of the ideas may be used as games; others are
intended to be humorous. Most of the ideas require little preparation—some photo-

copying, some supplies, and a few writing materials, and you'll be ready. The main point to remember for the introductions is to use them informally. Try these ideas as crowd breakers; allow the students to have fun, get up from their seats, interact, and begin the lesson on a light note.

Participation

The ideas presented under this section are designed to involve students with one of the main points of the lesson. Like the introduction, this section gets students up and moving and interacting with one another. The ideas under this section don't necessarily tie in directly to the thesis of the lesson, but are designed to set up the central point.

Observation

The ideas presented under this section are designed to let the students "see" part of the lesson. These ideas will help students make a visual connection with the lesson. Sometimes the observation will set up the instruction time and lead into the teaching. Other times the observation reinforces what's already been taught.

Instruction

The ideas presented under this section are designed to help you communicate a few biblical truths to your students. I realize you will be able to find additional interpretations of a selected passage. Use what fits best with your style, your beliefs, and your group. I don't claim to be a theologian. The presented truths are the answers I came up with when I asked myself, "Why is this in the Bible and what does it mean to students today?" These instructional ideas are intended to give you direction as distinct from being complete youth talks. If you want your students to investigate the Scripture text a bit further, use the extra questions in the *Digging In* and *Digging Deeper* features. These questions will encourage your students to dig into the text for the answers.

Application

The ideas presented under this section are designed to help students immediately apply the biblical truth that was taught. In some lessons, there are action steps for students to take or items they may bring home. The goal of this section is to help answer the "so what?" question and show how the lesson relates to students' lives.

Estimate your time

Each lesson is designed to be completed in approximately fifty minutes. Since each youth group and teaching setting varies, carefully read through each lesson and make any time adjustments you feel might be necessary. You may find that you can't use all the material within the time you have. That's okay! Use what works in the amount of time you have and save the remaining material for another meeting.

Take time to prepare

This book was written to cut down your preparation time, not eliminate it altogether. Read through each lesson at least a couple of hours prior to teaching it. Most of your preparation time will include reading the lesson, photocopying the handouts, and gathering a few materials. (If you have the same luck with copy machines as I do, don't wait until the last minute to copy your handouts.) These handouts will really add to the quality "feel" of each lesson.

Also, spend a few minutes thinking through the transitions from one section to the next (for example, from participation to instruction). Some of the transitions contain specific bridge comments, while others need you to provide the bridge sentence or instruction to make the flow more understandable.

Add your own creativity

Are you one of those people who claim that you don't have a creative bone in your body? Well, aside from that not being true, you can rest in the fact that the essence of creativity lies in your ability to copy these ideas and adapt them to your situation.

If you have some additional preparation time, spend it thinking through how you can take the provided ideas a step further with more personalized illustrations or applications.

Be flexible

If you experience a situation where a student or students begin to share a hurt or need some personal ministry time, be ready to adapt. If life change is happening during the participation section, don't force yourself into the instruction section. Let it go—even if you're running out of time. God may have a different agenda from yours. Being flexible allows God to work on his timing. I've found that most of God's "divine appointments" come at times I didn't plan. The goal of educating your students is to be effective, not necessarily efficient.

Adapt to your group size

Don't get caught in the trap of saying, "This won't work with the size of my group." Think through each section and brainstorm ways you can make an idea either bigger or smaller.

Keep God in the process

Let's face it, we can fool anyone about the depth of our spirituality. Well, anyone except God. You'll find greater wisdom, strength, and patience when you commit your role as a leader, and each of these lessons, to God. God doesn't expect you to be the greatest teacher ever; he doesn't even expect you to have your own life completely together. But God does want you to do the possible and have faith that he will do the impossible.

"We have this treasure in jars of clay to show that this all-surpassing power is from God and not from us" (II Corinthians 4:7).

Jesus Encounters Nathanael
Dealing with Doubt

John 1:43-51

Overview

This lesson is designed to show your students that Jesus is able to handle their honest questions and doubts. They need to know that God does not expect them to blindly commit their lives to him. Jesus is more than happy to prove himself to those who are searching.

Introduction (15 minutes)

This section provides a fun way to start your students thinking about when to believe or not to believe someone. It will help them realize that sometimes it is good be a doubter.

1) Have your students form groups of five or six people. (If your group is smaller, you may stay together as one group.)

2) Pass out a deck of playing cards to each group.

3) Tell your students that they will be playing a game called *I Doubt It.* (They may know this game by some other name.) The rules are as follows:

  a) Someone deals out all of the cards to the group members.

  b) Each player must play in turn, moving to the right of the dealer.

  c) The first player lays from one to four cards face-down in the middle of the circle, beginning with the ace. For example, the first player might say, "I am laying down two aces." The next player may choose to lay down three twos, and so on.

  d) If a player does not have the next consecutive card to lay down,

MATERIALS NEEDED

✔ Several decks of playing cards

✔ Pencils

✔ Copies of *Step by Step* (page 23)

✔ Copy of the video *Indiana Jones and the Last Crusade*

✔ Television

✔ VCR

✔ Copies of *Excuse Me But Can You Tell Me Where I'm Going?* (page 24)

DIGGING IN

1) Often people are on their guard when they first get to know someone. Look over John 1:43-51. In what ways did Jesus begin to remove Nathanael's barriers so that Nathanael could get closer to him?

2) Jesus knew something that Nathanael thought was a complete secret. What does this fact tell you about Jesus?

3) If you were in the presence of someone who knew every single thing about you, how would you feel? What would it take for you to be comfortable around that person?

he or she will need to fake as though he or she is laying down the correctly numbered card.

e) Immediately after a player has set down his or her cards, any other player may say, "I doubt it."

f) If the player has laid down the proper card(s), the doubter has to pick up all the cards in the middle. If the player was faking, he or she must pick up the cards in the middle.

g) The game continues until someone has sucessfully gotten rid of all of his or her cards.

4) After the game has finished, discuss with your students whether it paid for them to be a doubter in this game. Ask them why they think some people seemed to doubt more than others.

Instruction (10 minutes)

This section introduces the Scripture passage and helps your students understand that Jesus welcomed Nathanael's doubts.

1) Have someone read John 20:31, then say, "John says that the reason he wrote his gospel was to convince people who had doubts that Jesus was who he said he was. In the very first chapter John described someone who was skeptical of Jesus. As I read this story think about the series of events that convinced Nathanael to believe in Jesus."

2) Read John 1:43-51. Ask your students to identify specific incidents that caused Nathanael to get to know who Jesus really was. Write the steps on a whiteboard or easel as students state them. They should make the following observations:

a) Nathanael's friend believed in Jesus (vv. 43-44).

b) The friend told Nathanael about Jesus (v. 45).

c) Nathanael was skeptical as to whether Jesus was really who he said he was (v. 46).

d) Nathanael decided to investigate further (vv. 46-47).

e) Jesus proved himself (v. 48).

f) Nathanael committed himself to Jesus (v. 49).

g) Jesus encouraged Nathanael to keep checking him out (vv. 50-51).

3) Point out that Jesus was glad to deal with Nathanael's doubts and questions.

Observation (10 minutes)

This section helps your students to evaluate where they are on their journey toward trusting Jesus with their lives.

1) Say, "None of us travel the exact same journey as we try to understand who Jesus is and what difference he can make in our lives."

2) Hand out copies of *Step by Step* (page 23).

3) Ask your kids to review the events that brought Nathanael to Jesus.

4) Have your students fill out *Step by Step*, identifying the key events that have brought them to the place where they are now with Jesus.

5) After your students have completed *Step by Step*, have a few volunteers share the steps in their journeys. [**Note:** Some of your kids may realize that their journey is away from Jesus, or that they do not know Jesus at all. Let them know that it's okay to acknowlegde this. The point of the activity is to help your kids make an honest appraisal of the state of their spiritual journeys.]

Application (15 minutes)

This section points out that it is important for your students to thoroughly investigate who Jesus is before they decide to follow him. Encourage young people who are in the process of trusting Christ to express their doubts and allow Christ the opportunity to continue to prove himself.

1) Rent or borrow the video *Indiana Jones and the Last Crusade*.

DIGGING DEEPER

1) Notice John 1:50-51. Throughout the Bible, angels act as God's messengers. What do you think Jesus is trying to say about his role in the relationship between God and people?

2) What was Jesus offering Nathanael? Do you think this would be an attractive offer to Nathanael? Why or why not?

3) If someone offered you a direct two-way satellite linkup with God, would you take it? Why or why not?

2) Show the clip where Indiana Jones has to decide whether or not to step off the cliff, even though there is nothing visible to step on to.

3) Say, "In many ways, we are in the same position as Indiana Jones. It requires a step of faith for us to trust our lives to Jesus Christ and to live the way he asks us to."

4) Ask your students to close their eyes while you take them on a little journey. Read the story at the beginning of *Excuse Me, But Can You Tell Me Where I'm Going* (page 24)?

5) Pass out pencils and copies of *Excuse Me, But Can You Tell Me Where I'm Going?*

6) Have your students complete the questions.

7) After your students are done, say, "God will not frown on us for the questions we have. It is normal to investigate the things we have been told. Investigating allows us to make intelligent decisions."

8) Share honestly the times when you have doubted your faith. Close in prayer by asking God to reveal himself to your students as they continue to seek him.

STEP BY STEP

What key events in your life have helped you know more about Jesus? Starting from the point where you knew nothing at all about who Jesus is, identify key points on your personal journey.

EXCUSE ME,
BUT CAN YOU TELL ME WHERE I'M GOING?

Imagine that one morning you wake up and discover that you are in a strange and alien body. Everyone around you seems to be in the same situation. You are puzzled and confused. You're asking: Who am I? How did I get here? Why am I here? What am I supposed to be doing here? Am I stuck in this strange body forever?

You must find someone with the answers. You jump up and run around, desperately searching for someone who can give you direction. There are many other strange creatures around you. Some of them seem just as confused as you are. Others are trying to help you. You listen to one, and then another. Each of them acts as if it knows the answer.

You begin to wonder if this is all one big trick. Time is racing. You don't know how long you might have to live. For all you know, your body might self-destruct at any time.

You tell yourself that there must be someone who is in charge. Someone who set up this whole thing. But where is this person? Who is this person?

You may not realize it, but that is the situation you are in right now. You may not have thought about it, but these questions are still waiting to be answered.

Jesus Christ is standing down at the corner calling out, "Follow me, I'll show you where to go." But you may not be sure he can be trusted. You may have some doubts. Maybe you have even started to follow him a little bit, but now you are having second thoughts.

What doubts do you have about Jesus?

Are you willing to bring those doubts to Jesus and give him the opportunity to prove himself to you? Why or why not?

24

Lesson
Jesus Encounters the Money Changers
Respecting God

John 2:13-25

Overview

This lesson is designed to teach students that they live in the presence of God. It will help them to realize that God is aware of and concerned about everything they do and say. This lesson will challenge your students to give God the respect he deserves.

Introduction (10 minutes)

This section gets students thinking about the way the name of God is used in everyday life, often in vulgar and profane ways.

1) Tell your students that you are conducting a survey to find out what is the most commonly-used expression about God at their school.
2) Pass out copies of *Big Man on Campus* (page 29) and give students time to rate which expressions are used the most frequently.
3) After everyone has filled out the worksheet, tally the results; then rank the expressions according to the kids' responses.
4) Ask your students why they think the name of God is so popular. Say, "Do you think people are really thinking about who God is when they use his name? Why do you think God's name is so often used as a swear word?"

Participation (15 minutes)

This section will help make students aware of what it is like to have an audience that notices all that they do. It will also introduce the

DIGGING IN

1) Read John 2:18-25. Compare the way the Jews (vv. 18-20), the disciples (v. 22), and the people (v. 23) responded to what Jesus did. What do you think were the attitudes and motives of each group?

2) Jesus' actions caught everyone's attention. Does God ever use circumstances in your life to get your attention? Explain.

3) Notice verses 24 and 25. It seems as though some of the people in this story missed an important opportunity to hear from God. What do you think kept Jesus from opening up to those who were following him? How can you make it easier for God to speak to you?

Scripture passage in a dramatic way.

1) Announce that you are going to play a game that will help your students feel what it is like for others to notice their each and every move.

2) Set up a card table with *Trivial Pursuit.* (If this game is unavailable, find another game with the same purpose.) Begin playing the game, with these additional instructions:

a) Have students divide into two teams and appoint a team spokesperson.

b) Give each team member a noisemaker (whistles, bells, horns, rattles, keys, etc.).

c) Tell your students that whenever the opposing team answers a question incorrectly, the team spokesperson should stand up and shout "You're wrong!" The other team members should then make a racket with their noisemakers.

d) Whenever their own team answers correctly all the team members should stand up and use their noisemakers to applaud.

e) If there are students who are not playing, instruct them to cheer all correct answers and jeer at all incorrect answers regardless of which team is answering.

3) After the game has been going for five or ten minutes, have someone storm into your room and ask indignantly, "What do you guys think you are doing?!" This person should proceed to turn the card table over, sending the cards and game pieces flying.

4) After regathering game pieces and collecting the noisemakers, have a few willing students share what it felt like to be noticed every time they answered. Get their reactions to the rather dramatic end to the game.

Instruction (10 minutes)

This section will help students to realize that almighty God is their unseen audience and that they live their lives in front of him.

1) Say, "In the game it was obvious when people were pleased or displeased with your actions. We are about to read a story where Jesus turns over tables and sends things flying. Jesus makes people aware of how they are acting in the presence of God."

2) Read John 2:13-17 aloud and then make the following observations:

a) The vendors and money changers where doing business directly in front of the temple where God was worshipped, but seemed totally unaware of him.

b) Nothing disturbed Jesus more than when he saw people choose to disrespect God.

c) Jesus demanded that the money changers stop what they were doing and consider how their actions reflected on God's reputation.

4) Ask your students to share any other things they may have observed from the story.

Observation (5 minutes)

This section will provide a fun way for students to think about how much God deserves their respect.

1) Read the riddles from *So Big You Just Can't Ignore It* (page 30) one at a time. Allow students to guess the answers after each question, then give the punch line.

2) Point out to your students that when we realize who God is, it is foolish for us to try to pretend that he is not right there with us, wherever we go and whatever we do.

DIGGING DEEPER

1) For the Jews, the temple in Jerusalem was considered to be the dwelling place of God. Jesus said in John 4:21-24 that soon the place of true worship would change. What change was he talking about? How might this change affect the way you relate to God?

2) Jesus chased the money changers early in his ministry. What did he do several years later near the end of his ministry (Matthew 21:12-13)?

3) What can we learn from these two incidents about our responsibility in building our relationship with God?

Application (10 minutes)

This section demonstrates to your students that being aware of God and respecting him are things they can choose to do or not to do. They are encouraged to allow God to affect all the compartments of their lives.

1) Explain to your students that although God wants to affect every part of their lives, the choice is still up to them.

2) Give each student a copy of the handout *Turning the Tables* (pages 31–32).

3) Have students choose one table to write about.

4) After they have finished writing about one table, encourage them to take the worksheet home and think about how their activities and attitudes might change, knowing that God is with them. Close in prayer.

BIG MAN ON CAMPUS

You may hear the following expressions a lot at school. They all invoke the name of God. Place a number from one to ten beside each name. Give the number one to the expression you hear most frequently and number 10 to the expression you hear least frequently.

_____ God almighty

_____ For Christ's sake

_____ God

_____ Jesus Christ

_____ Oh my God

_____ Jesus

_____ God d—— it

_____ God bless you

_____ God help you

_____ For God's sake

So Big You Just Can't Ignore It

Question: How can you tell when a charging bull has been through a jewelry store?

Answer: All of the nose rings are missing.

Question: What do you get when you put a grizzly bear and a mountain lion in a room?

Answer: Out of there.

Question: What do sharks do for fun?

Answer: Look for a fishing pole with a human attached to the other end.

Question: What should you say if you run into a huge guy with a gun in a dark alley?

Answer: Excuse me.

Question: What do you feed a 600–pound parrot?

Answer: Anything it asks for.

Question: What is more scary than coming across a giant meat–eating dinosaur?

Answer: Coming across a giant meat–eating dinosaur with a growling stomach.

Question: How can you tell if an elephant has been in your refrigerator?

Answer: By the footprints in the peanut butter.

Turning the Tables

Think about these different tables in your life and what activities they represent. Ask yourself: What could I do differently to show God that I respect him while I am at this table? Are there any activities I do at this table that ignore God's presence in my life?

Kitchen Table
(Interaction with my family)

Activities that ignore God   Activities that honor God

_____   _____

_____   _____

_____   _____

Pool Table
(Recreational activities)

Activities that ignore God   Activities that honor God

_____   _____

_____   _____

_____   _____

Cafeteria Table
(Interaction with friends at school)

Activities that ignore God   Activities that honor God

_____   _____

_____   _____

_____   _____

Table of Contents
(Things you read, things you
listen to, and things you watch)

Activities that ignore God | Activities that honor God

_____ | _____

_____ | _____

_____ | _____

Multiplication
Tables
(Classes and homework)

Activities that ignore God | Activities that honor God

_____ | _____

_____ | _____

_____ | _____

Timetable
(Things you do in your spare time)

Activities that ignore God | Activities that honor God

_____ | _____

_____ | _____

_____ | _____

Jesus Encounters Nicodemus
Receiving New Life in Christ

John 3:1–36

Overview

This lesson is designed to help students to see that when they put their faith in Christ, it radically changes who they are on the inside. It helps them to realize that just as physical birth begins a whole new world of human interaction, spiritual birth allows them to experience a vital relationship with God.

Introduction (10-15 minutes)

This section introduces the subject of birth and gets students thinking about how birth is a miraculous event.

1) If you are feeling brave, begin the class by showing your students the first few minutes of the movie *Look Who's Talking*. This part of the movie shows hundreds of sperm racing toward an unfertilized egg like a pack of children just released from school for summer vacation. This will certainly get your students' attention and start them thinking about the birth process. [**Note:** It may be wise to check with your pastor and some key parents ahead of time before using this clip. If you decide not to use this clip, just start with # 2.]

2) Say something like: "Babies are born every day, and yet most of us never really stop to think about how amazing the whole process of conception, pregnancy, and birth really is." Announce to your students that you have a "birth quiz" to give them. Hand out copies of *I Was Born That Way* (page 37). Allow your students to guess the answer to each question. You may want to copy this sheet on a transparency and reveal

MATERIALS NEEDED

- ✔ Copy of the video *Look Who's Talking*
- ✔ Television
- ✔ VCR
- ✔ Copies of *I Was Born That Way* (page 37)
- ✔ Overhead projector (optional)
- ✔ Baby pictures
- ✔ Party hats, balloons, horns, streamers (optional)
- ✔ Birthday cake
- ✔ Birthday candles and matches
- ✔ Ice cream
- ✔ Paper plates
- ✔ Plastice forks and spoons
- ✔ Napkins

DIGGING IN

1) Nicodemus is introduced to us for the first time in John, chapter three. Look carefully at John 3:1-2. What do you learn about Nicodemus from these verses? What is it Nicodemus wants from Jesus? How would you describe the way the conversation is going between Jesus and Nicodemus in verses 9-12?

2) Nicodemus was obviously an intelligent man. Why do you think he was having such a hard time accepting and understanding what Jesus was saying? Why do you think Nicodemus waited until night to approach Jesus?

3) Read John 3:16. Why do you think some people have trouble accepting such a simple concept? What barriers have you had to overcome to accept this promise?

Participation (10 minutes)

This section moves your students from the general subject of birth to thinking about their personal birth experience.

1) Open by saying. "While none of us remembers our own birth, we can all be sure that it happened. Let's talk about it."

2) Break your students into groups of two or three. Give groups five minutes to discuss anything they have been told by their parents or other people about their birth.

3) Have your students return to the large group. Have a few willing students share anything they would like to about their births.

4) You may want to pass around your own baby picture or, if you are a parent, a picture of one of your children on the day he or she was born.

Instruction (10 minutes)

This section introduces the Scripture for this lesson. It helps the students see that spiritual birth is as real and miraculous as physical birth.

1) Select three student volunteers to give a dramatic reading (the more dramatic the better) of John 3:1-12. The characters are the Narrator, Nicodemus, and Jesus. After the reading, make the following observations:

a) Just as physical birth is required to enter the world, spiritual birth is required for a relationship with God (3:3).

b) We cannot take any credit for our physical births. In the same way, we have to admit that we cannot reach God ourselves. Spiritual birth is an act of the Holy Spirit (3:6).

c) Just as we had to depend on the stories from our parents about our birth, we must depend on the words of Jesus about our spiritual birth (3:11-13).

2) Ask your students if any of them remember when their parents told them the facts of life. Tell them that in John 3:16, Jesus tells Nicodemus the spiritual facts of life. Invite a volunteer to explain this verse to the rest of the class as though he or she were talking to a child. Listen to make sure they include the following observations:

a) God loves you.
b) Jesus died for you.
c) You must put your faith in Jesus.
d) You will receive life with God forever.

Observation (10 minutes)

This section helps your students realize that a supernatural birth has actually taken place in their lives if they have put their trust in Christ.

1) Tell your students that they are all going to participate in a guessing game.
2) One at a time, have your group vote on whether they think each person in the group is a morning person, an evening person, or neither.
3) After each vote, have that particular student reveal his or her preference. As preferences are revealed, have students stand with like-minded souls.
4) After students have returned to their seats, say, "Was there any way to tell whether a person is an evening person or a morning person just by looking at them? Jesus tells us that the same is true of those who have been born again. The change takes place on the inside. Christians become 'light–lovers.'"
5) Read John 3:19-21, and make the following observations:

a) Jesus is comparing someone who lives in darkness to someone who is comfortable allowing sin to continue in their lives.
b) Jesus is comparing someone who comes to the light to someone who is more comfortable admitting their sin and receiving forgiveness.
c) Jesus is saying that if we have been born again, something has changed on the inside. We can live in the darkness by hiding our sin, but it no longer feels right. We are really only comfortable when we allow the light of confession and forgiveness to shine on our lives.

Application (5-10 minutes)

This section helps students experience the reality of their spiritual birth with a celebration.

1) Give each of your students a party hat and whistle.

2) Bring out a birthday cake with two candles. One candle represents physical birthdays; the other represents spiritual birthdays.

3) Serve ice cream and cake, and encourage students to share the circumstances that surrounded their spiritual birthdays.

4) Give students who have never trusted Christ an opportunity to talk with you about being born into God's family.

I WAS BORN THAT WAY

1. What is the age of the oldest mother ever known to give birth?

2. What was the weight of the largest baby born?

3. What is the greatest number of children officially recorded as being born to one woman?

4. What was the weight of the smallest living baby?

5. What is the highest number of children born at a single birth?

6. What is the longest time interval between the birth of twins?

7. What is the fastest recorded birth of triplets?

ANSWERS TO I WAS BORN THAT WAY

1. The oldest mother was Sarah, wife of Abraham as recorded in the book of Genesis. The oldest reported age of a pregnacy in recent history is 63.

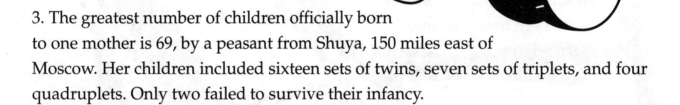

2. The biggest baby born to healthy mother was a boy, weighing 22 lb. 8 oz. He was born to Signora Carmelina Fedele of Aversa, Italy in September 1955.

3. The greatest number of children officially born to one mother is 69, by a peasant from Shuya, 150 miles east of Moscow. Her children included sixteen sets of twins, seven sets of triplets, and four quadruplets. Only two failed to survive their infancy.

4. A premature baby girl weighing 9.9 ounces was reported to have been born in 1989 at the Loyola University Medical Center in Chicago, Illinois.

5. The highest number of babies reported born at a single birth were ten; two males and eight females at Bacacay, Brazil on April 22, 1946.

6. Mrs. Danny Petrungaro of Rome, Italy gave birth normally to a girl, Diana, on December 22 1987, but the other twin, Monica, was delivered by cesarean on January 27, 1988, 36 days later.

7. Bradley, Christopher, and Carmon were born naturally to Mrs. James E. Duck of Memphis Tennessee in two minutes on March 21, 1977.

Information obtained from *Guiness Book of World Records,* 1995, Guiness Publishing Ltd. 1994. pp. 59-61

Lesson 4
Jesus Encounters a Nobleman's Son and a Crippled Man
Coping with Crisis

John 4:43-5:18

Overview

This lesson is designed to teach your students that they can trust Jesus with the difficulties they face in their lives. In this incident from John, Jesus contradicts the popular belief that God is too busy to be bothered with the problems people face. Your students will discover that Jesus is ready and willing to be their very best friend.

Introduction (10-15 minutes)

This exercise is a fun and interesting way to get your students thinking about the qualities of a true friend.

1) Tell the students that you would like three volunteers to conduct a short telephone survey. The survey is about friendship.

2) Pass out a copy of *Reach Out and Touch Someone* (page 43) to each volunteer.

3) Have a fourth person randomly select numbers from the phone book for each volunteer to call. It will be more exciting if the interviewers do not know the people they are calling. (Just make sure it is not too early in the morning!)

4) Have the volunteers take turns calling the randomly selected phone numbers. They are to follow the instructions on the handouts as they conduct the interview. You may want to use a speaker phone so that everyone can hear both ends of the conversation. Allow each volunteer to each make one or two calls.

5) If you didn't use a speaker phone, have students report back the answers people gave about friendship.

MATERIALS NEEDED

✔ Three copies of *Reach Out and Touch Someone* (page 43)

✔ Pencils

✔ A telephone (speaker phone if available)

✔ Current phone book

✔ Copies of *What's the Difference?* (page 44)

✔ Posterboard

✔ Tape

✔ Marker

✔ Three copies of *Dear Jesus* (page 45)

✔ Blank greeting card or index card for each member of the group

DIGGING IN

1) Review the two stories in John 4:43-5:18. In what way was each man required to demonstrate his trust in Jesus?

2) Why do you think Jesus required a demonstration of faith from each man? Were there any risks involved in trusting Jesus? Explain.

3) Which do you feel would have been more risky for these men—to trust Jesus or just hope for the best? Why?

4) Suppose you were to interview these two men. What advice do you think they would give you about trusting Jesus?

6) Ask students if there is anything they feel should be added to the answers people gave.

Instruction (20 minutes)

This section introduces the Scriptures for this lesson. It helps students see that Jesus is interested in helping anyone, no matter what the person's status. These passages demonstrate that Jesus has the qualities of a true friend.

1) Hand out a copy of *What's the Difference?* (page 44) to each group member.

2) Have your students to work in groups of twos or threes. Have each group come up with as many differences and similarities as they can in five minutes from these two stories (John 4:43-54 and John 5:1-18).

3) When time is up, have a volunteer from one group read their list of *similarities*. Be sure your students pick up the following observations:

a) Both people were facing problems they could not solve themselves.

b) Both admitted they needed help.

c) Both people had to take Jesus at his word.

d) Both received help from Jesus.

4) Have someone from another group read their list of *differences*. Be sure to add the following differences if they have been overlooked:

a) One person was in a respected position while the other was disrespected.

b) Parents supported the son; the other apparently was alone.

c) One person had recently run into problems while the other person had had problems for a long time.

d) Jesus used different methods to help each person.

5) On a whiteboard or a piece of posterboard, write on the top: "Who is Jesus? What is he like?"

6) Have students answer these questions as they skim the two stories again. Have someone write down the answers group members came up with. If missed by your students, add the following observations to the list:

    a) Jesus takes the time to help hurting people.
    b) Jesus does not force himself on anyone.
    c) Jesus treats each person as an individual.

7) Challenge the class to see if anyone thinks he or she can use all of the statements about Jesus that the group wrote down in one sentence.

Observation (15 minutes)

This section allows the students to put themselves in the shoes of other teenagers. It helps them picture how Jesus could make a positive difference in the lives of young people.

1) Select three volunteers. Give each volunteer a copy of *Dear Jesus* (page 45). Have each person, one at a time, read one of the three letters.

2) Stop after each person reads his or her letter. Ask your students what they think Jesus might do for or say to this person in light of what they just discovered about Jesus from the two stories. Encourage them to look at the lists to remind themselves what Jesus is like.

3) Allow your students to struggle for a while with these difficult situations. Let your students know that often there is no easy answer. Assure your students that Jesus is concerned for each of them individually. He wants what is best for us. Sometimes we just have to trust him to answer in his own way and his own time. Let them know that sometimes God uses other people to meet needs. [**Note:** This lesson may bring to the surface some difficult life issues in some of your kids. Be available in case a young person wants to talk after the meeting, or at some other time you can schedule.]

Application (5 minutes)

This section gives your students a chance to personalize their relationship with Jesus Christ.

1) Give each student a blank greeting card or an index card.

2) Ask them to think about a crisis they are facing now or may face in the future.

3) Offer the students a chance to write a brief personal message to Jesus, asking for his help in facing this crisis.

4) Suggest to your kids to take the card home and place it somewhere they will see it daily. This card can serve as a reminder of their relationship with Jesus Christ.

Reach Out and Touch Someone

1) Interviewer: Hello, my name is _____. I am part of the youth group at _____. We are conducting a brief survey on friendship. Would you be willing to answer two questions for us?

Question # 1: What do you consider the most important qualities in a friend?

Question #2: How can you tell if someone is a true friend?

Thank you for your time.

What's the Difference?

Compare the two stories found in John 4:43-54 and John 5:1-18.

List as many differences as you can find between these two events.

List as many similarities as you can find between these two stories.

Dear Jesus

Dear Jesus,

My name is Ted. I am a senior in high school. My dad is an alcoholic. Every night when I come home I never know what to expect. The whole family is scared of him, especially my little sister. She is only eight. Sometimes I wish I could take her and leave and never come back. Can you help me?

Dear Jesus,

I am a ninth grader. My name is Nancy. I have felt like a clod all of my life. I have friends, but no one really likes me. If anyone knew what I was really like they probably wouldn't even talk to me. Sometimes I wonder if God made a mistake when he made me. Is there any hope for me?

Dear Jesus,

My name is Carol. I am in my second year of high school. I have so much pressure; sometimes I feel like I might explode. My parents expect me to stay on the honor roll. I'm in the band and trying out for basketball. I keep getting distracted at school because my mom and dad are having problems. I feel like I have the weight of the world on my shoulders. I just don't know where to turn.

Jesus Encounters the Crowd
Accepting God's Incredible Gift

John 6:46-60

Overview
This lesson is designed to help students realize that the cleansing of their sin cost God the life of his son.

Introduction (10 minutes)
This section introduces the subject of sin in a entertaining way. It is designed to keep your students thinking about their need for spiritual cleansing throughout the lesson.

1) Start out by saying something like, "Most of us probably don't spend much time thinking about the penalty for our sins, but that is today's topic. We are going to play a little game to get us thinking about various types of sin. "

2) Pass out a washable crayon marker to each student.

3) Explain the game, using the following instructions:

   a) The object is for each player to have as many sins as possible written on his or her hands and forearms.

   b) When the game begins, each person goes around the room, and asks others to write out the name of any particular sin on his or her hands or forearms.

   c) No one can have the same person write on his or her arm more than once.

   d) The game lasts just 60 seconds.

MATERIALS NEEDED

✔ Washable crayon markers

✔ Small prizes

✔ Radio, tape recorder, and blank cassette tape

✔ Tray, glass pitchter, Dixie cups, and toothpicks

✔ Tomato juice, ham cubes

✔ A large bowl, towels, and several bars of soap

✔ Scriptures from *The Price is Right* (page 51) on paper strips or index cards

✔ Pieces of scarlet thread

✔ Plastic fangs (optional)

DIGGING IN

1) Earlier in John 6, Jesus had fed five thousand people. The crowds were still following him, hoping to see another miracle and to get fed again. Jesus contrasts the crowd's desire for physical food with their need for spiritual food. Carefully read through John 6:46-60 again; then draw a chart that compares the differences and similarities between physical food and the spiritual food referred to in this passage.

2) Why do you think it was easy for the crowd to accept the physical food Jesus offered, but difficult for them to accept the spiritual food he offered?

3) We like to think that we can take care of ourselves. How might self–reliance keep us from appreciating Christ's sacrifice?

4) When the game is over, find out who collected the most sins. Have the person with the most sins read them to the rest of the students. (Award a small prize to the winner.)

5) Have other students share any additional sins listed on their arms that haven't been mentioned.

6) Tell your students that they will have an opportunity to wash the marker off later in the lesson.

Participation (5–10 minutes)

This section encourages your students to listen and think about things that are difficult to understand.

1) Before the lesson, tape record five-second sound bites from ten to fifteen different songs played on a radio station popular with most of your students. (You may want to use several different radio stations, depending on the diversity of your group.)

2) Explain to your students that you will be playing short sections of various songs you recorded off the radio.

3) When each sound bite is played, have students stand up if they know the artist and song title.

4) Award a prize to the person with the most correct answers—a package of Pop Rocks™ (a brand of candy that explodes in your mouth) or another appropriate prize.

Instruction (15 minutes)

This section introduces the Scripture to your students while helping them vividly picture what Jesus is saying. It may cause them to feel some of the repulsion the Jews must have felt by what Jesus said.

1) Say, "We just saw that it is important to listen carefully when we are hearing something difficult to understand. The people listening to Jesus in John 6 had a difficult time understanding and accepting what he was saying. Let's see how well we do."

2) Tell your students that you will be serving a snack to anyone who wants it while the passage is being read.

3) Have a volunteer begin reading John 6:46-60.

4) As the volunteer is reading, bring in a tray with a glass pitcher of tomato juice, Dixie cups, and a plate of ham cubes with toothpicks in them.

5) Move around the room offering refreshments to anyone that wants some.

6) When the passage has been read, have a few willing students share how they felt about being offered the snack while this particular passage was being read.

7) Then say, "There are several short observations we can make from this passage:

"a) Jesus was freely offering eternal life to anyone that would accept it.

"b) The gift of eternal life cost God his son and Jesus his life.

"c) Only by accepting the bloody sacrifice of Jesus Christ can we be right with God."

Observation (15 minutes)

This section helps your students appreciate what Christ's death accomplished for them.

1) Bring a large bowl filled with warm water into the middle of the room. Set several towels and bars of soap around the bowl.

2) Place a stack of paper slips or index cards with the Scriptures from the *The Price is Right* (page 51) beside the bowl.

3) Ask your students to wash the marker off their hands and forearms in the following manner:

a) One or two students should approach the bowl at a time.

b) Each student picks up a paper slip or card and reads it aloud.

c) Students should then wash the marker off their hands and arms and sit back down.

d) After they are seated, one or two more students should come up and follow the same instructions.

4) After everyone has washed off their sins, have a few willing students share any feelings they had about forgiveness as they washed their arms.

Application (5 minutes)

This section provides students with reminders of the sacrifice that was made for their sin.

1) Tell your students that you are giving them something to remind them of how much God loves them and of the price he paid for them.

2) Pass out a piece of scarlet thread to each student. Tell them to tie their pieces of thread around their wrists and wear them for a week, or keep the thread pieces someplace where they will see them during the week.

 Option

Hand out plastic fangs as a reminder to your students that they need Jesus' blood for forgiveness. (Use this option at your own risk!)

3) Close by thanking God for sacrificing his son for us.

$ The Price is Right $

Make several copies of this sheet, then cut it into strips. If you prefer, copy the passages onto index cards.

Isaiah 1:18b
Though your sins are like scarlet, they shall be as white as snow; though they are red like crimson they shall be like wool.

Revelation 1:5b
To him who loves us and has freed us from our sins by his own blood.

I Corinthians 6:11b
But you were washed, you were sanctified, you were justified in the name of the Lord Jesus Christ and by the Spirit of our God.

I John 1:9
If we confess our sins, he is faithful and just and will forgive us our sins and purify us from all unrighteousness.

Matthew 26:28
This is my blood of the covenant, which is poured out for many for the forgiveness of sins.

Lesson 6
Jesus Encounters a Blind Man
Accepting God's Love

John 9:1–41

Overview

This lesson is designed to help your students realize that they are accepted and loved by God. It focuses on the freedom that comes when they can be honest about who they are with God, themselves, and others.

Introduction (5-10 minutes)

This game provides a fun way for your students to experience what it feels like to put up a false front.

1) Tell your students that they are going to play a game that will test their vocabulary.

2) Flip open a dictionary and read the first difficult word you find on the page.

3) Have three students do their best to define the word. The object is for each student to convince everyone else that *he* or *she* has the correct definition.

4) Allow the other students to vote on who they think has the correct definition.

5) Read the correct defintion. If you want, award the student who received the most votes a prize for his or her ability to convince others.

6) Repeat the game with other students if time permits.

7) When you are finished, say something like this: "It can be difficult to pretend to know something when we really have no idea. In our lesson today, we will see several examples of people who try to pretend to be

MATERIALS NEEDED

✔ Dictionary

✔ Small prize

✔ Don Francisco recording of the song *I Can See* or another appropriate song (optional)

✔ Tape player

✔ Cassette tape with prerecorded answers from *Who Am I?* (see page 55, #3)

✔ Copies of *Who Am I?* (page 56)

✔ Overhead projector and transparency (optional)

✔ Marker for overhead projector (optional)

✔ Copies of *Satisfaction Guaranteed* (page 57)

53

DIGGING IN

1) Look over John 9:6-7 and John 9:35-39. What can you learn about the blind man's position in the community? Besides healing him, in what ways did Jesus show this man respect?

2) Why do you think that Jesus went to such effort to make contact with this man? What do Jesus actions say about God's value of human beings?

3) If we measured our value by the standards we see in advertisements, how would we feel about ourselves? How can this story help us look at ourselves differently?

something in order to feel accepted and worthwhile."

Instruction (10-15 minutes)

This section introduces the Scripture. It allows your students to step into the blind man's shoes and experience what it feels like to encounter Jesus. This passage shows that God had a positive purpose for allowing this man to be born blind.

1) Have students volunteer to play parts in a short skit. The parts include Jesus, the blind man, the disciples, and the neighbors.
    a) Tell them to listen carefully as you read John 9:1-12 because they will not be using scripts.
    b) After reading the passage, have your volunteers act out the scene based on what they remember.

2) When the skit is finished, ask your students what they think the blind man may have been feeling during this encounter. If you have the recording, have your kids listen to *I Can See* by Don Francisco or another approriate song while they ponder what the blind man must have felt like. Some of the feelings your students might come up with are fear, hope, value, and joy.

Observation (15-20 minutes)

This section examines several types of people in John 9 who attempted to bring value and meaning to their lives on their own. This section shows that people are better off when they acknowledge their weakness and trust Jesus to accept them anyway.

1) Let your students know that in a few minutes they will be hearing from three special guests. They will need to guess who the guests are.
2) Tell your students that they have two minutes to study John 9:13-34 and familiarize themselves with the primary characters.

3) Before your lesson, record three different adults reading the three different parts on the *Who Am I?* handout (page 56). Play these recordings now, one at a time.

4) After each recording, pause and ask your students to identify whom they think the character represents and why. (It may add a little more fun if you record the voices of adults the kids would recognize.)

　　a) Character #1 represents the attitude of the blind man's parents (see John 9:20-23).
　　b) Character #2 represents the attitude of one of the Pharisees (see John 9:28-34).
　　c) Character #3 represents the attitude of the man born blind (see John 9:24-27).

5) Now hand out copies of *Who Am I?* or, if you wish, make a transparency of this sheet and display it on the overhead.

6) Ask your students how they would answer the last two questions on the bottom of *Who Am I?* Help them to see that:

　　a) All of us are spiritually blind when we think we are sufficient to handle life on our own.
　　b) There is nothing wrong with having friends, being physically attractive, or being intelligent, but each of those things only brings temporary satisfaction.
　　c) Only the formerly blind man could truly see because he realized that apart from Jesus life was meaningless.

Application (5 minutes)

This section helps the students to consider what they look to for self esteem. It shows them that they do not have to impress God. He loves them just as they are.

1) Hand out copies of *Satisfaction Guaranteed* (page 57).
2) Have them fill in the blanks to personalize the guarantee.
3) Let your students know that what they write will not need to be shared with the class.
4) Close by sharing your own personalized guarantee with your students or allowing one volunteer to share his or hers.
5) Ask your students to take the guarantee home and read it over once before they go to bed. Tell them to keep it someplace accessible. Suggest that they pull it out and read it during times they may be feeling worthless or discouraged.

Who Am I?

 All my life I've tried to fit in. I just want to hang out with my friends and not cause any problems. Being accepted by my peer group is important to me. Who am I?

 I have always tried to do the very best I could with my life. My value comes from the fact that I try to be all that I can be. Because of my efforts I am more knowledgeable than most people my age. This will allow me to be in a better position in society. My importance comes from my accomplishments. Who am I?

 I have always felt that physically, I could not measure up to everyone else. Until recently I considered this a great disadvantage. Now I realize that I was made the way I am for a purpose. My physical weakness was not a punishment. It opened my eyes to my need for Jesus. I may have never seen my need of him if I had not had this difficulty. Who am I?

In John 9:39b Jesus said: "The blind will see and those who see will become blind." What do you think he meant by that?

Consider what the three people above said about themselves. Which of them would Jesus consider to be blind? Which of them would be able to see? Why?

Satisfaction Guaranteed

Your name _____

Area you feel most inadequate in:
_____ Friendships
_____ Accomplishments
_____ Intelligence
_____ Physical health
_____ Physical attractiveness
_____ Dynamic personality
_____ Athletic ability
_____ Other:_____

Personal Guarantee from Your Designer

John 9:1-3 Personalized

Jesus sees _____ (your name) just as you are, with all your

insecurities. Others may say to him: "Jesus, if _____ (your name)

had more_____ (your inadequacy) would

_____ (your name) be more acceptable to you?" Jesus

answers, "No, not at all. More _____ (your inadequacy)

would not make me accept _____ (your name) any more than

I already do. I made _____ (your name) just the way I wanted

_____ (your name) to be. Because _____ (your name)

has a relationship with me, _____ (your name) is free to be

_____ (your name). When people see _____ (your name),

they may want that kind of freedom and acceptance also."

Forever your Savior,

Jesus Christ

Lesson 7

Jesus Encounters Mary and Martha
Facing Death

John 10:40–11:46

Overview
This lesson is designed to show your students that Jesus is worthy of their trust because he has power over death.

Introduction (5 minutes)
This section starts your students thinking about how many ways people use the word *dead*.

1) Divide into two teams.
2) Give each team a pencil and paper. Then say, "In the next sixty seconds, write down as many expressions that use some form of the word *dead* (dying, die, death) in them as you can think of."
3) When time is up, bring both teams together and have each team read the expressions it came up with. Teams should cross off duplicate expressions.
4) The team with the most expressions is the winner. Ask everyone to pause for a moment of silence in honor of their dead expressions.

Observation (15 minutes)
This section is designed to cause your students to think about the ugly reality of death.

1) Ask your students to split into twos or threes.
2) Give each twosome or threesome a large sheet of drawing paper

MATERIALS NEEDED

✔ Pencils and paper

✔ Large sketch pad

✔ Colored markers or crayons

✔ Copies of *The Jerusalem Journal* (page 63)

✔ Copies of *Dear Diary* (page 64)

✔ Copies of *Spies R Us* (page 65)

✔ Index cards

✔ Several rolls of Lifesaver candies

✔ Copies of *Jesus the Ultimate Lifesaver* (page 66)

DIGGING IN

1) Skim over the story of Lazarus again. It would have been much simpler for Jesus to have healed Lazarus in the first place. Why did Jesus wait until Lazarus died to deal with the problem?

2) Notice John 11:38-44. Why do you think Jesus made such a big public production out of this event?

3) Have you ever wanted your prayers answered right this minute? What can you learn from the story of Mary, Martha, and Lazarus about what God thinks is most important?

from a sketch pad and several colored markers or crayons.
3) Ask them to take about five minutes to make posters that symbolize death. Tell them to include symbols that illustrate any emotions and experiences that are usually connected with death.
4) After they have finished making their posters, allow each twosome or threesome to display their poster and explain its meaning.

Instruction (15 minutes)
This section is designed to help your students understand that Jesus is even more powerful than death. Jesus is the one person that they can trust with their soul after they die.

1) Introduce the Scripture passage by saying, "Many of us avoid talking about or thinking about it because death causes negative emotions such as pain, sorrow, and fear. In the story we are about to look at, Jesus intentionally allows a close friend to die in order to teach people the truth about death."
2) Split your students into twos and threes.
3) Give one third of the twosomes or threesomes *The Jerusalem Journal* (page 63). Give another third of the groups *Dear Diary* (page 64). Give the last third of the groups *Spies R Us* (page 65—see note on page 64).
4) Allow five minutes for the groups to complete their worksheets.
5) When everyone has finished, have each group share their report. Make sure that all groups share in order to have a complete picture of what happened in this story.
6) Make the following observations:

a) Even though the death of Lazarus was tragic for his friends and relatives, Jesus used this event to bring honor to God.
b) Jesus knew the death of his friend Lazarus was a deep loss to those around him. He cried about the loss just like everyone else.

c) Jesus Christ has power over even death. Those that believe in him can have confidence in his power to raise them from the dead someday.

Participation (10 minutes)

This section makes the central point of the lesson: A person can only escape permanent death by having a relationship with the ultimate Life Giver—Jesus Christ.

1) Tell your students that you are about to play a game called *Live or Die*. Give your students the following instructions:

a) The object of the game is to meet the Life Giver before you die.

b) Hand out an index card to each person. All of the cards should be blank, except for two cards. One of these cards has a D on it; the other, an L. The person that receives the card with D on it is Death. The person that receives the card with an L on it is the Life Giver. No one is to reveal what is on his or her card.

d) Once everyone has a card, the game begins. Everyone must maintain eye contact with the other players in the game.

e) The person with the Death card kills people by winking at them. The Life Giver gives people life by wrinkling his or her nose at them.

f) If a person is killed, he or she should wait a few seconds, and then die a dramatic death. If people are given life, they should wait a few seconds, and then stand up and claim, "I'm invincible." The people with the marked cards cannot be killed or receive life.

g) No one is to reveal who the Life Giver or Death are.

h) The game continues until everyone is either dead or invincible.

2) After a few rounds, remind students that Jesus is the ultimate Life Giver. Knowing him allows them to gain the final victory over death.

Application (5-10 minutes)

This section is designed to help your students apply the fact of Jesus' power over death to their own situations.

1) Open several rolls of Lifesaver candies.

2) Have each student take a Lifesaver and pass the roll to the next person, and so on.

3) Pass out copies of *Jesus the Ultimate Lifesaver* (page 66) to your students and have them complete the worksheet.

4) When your students have completed the worksheet, have a few volunteers share their answers to the questions.

5) Be sure to tell your students that you will be available if they have any questions about how to accept Jesus personally as *their* Ultimate Lifesaver.

THE JERUSALEM
Journal
FINAL EDITION

★★★★★ ★★★★★

Assignment: You are a group of reporters from the *Jerusalem Journal.* Your assignment is to cover the activities of Jesus while he is staying about 15 to 20 miles north of Bethany. Use John 10:40–11:16 as your source of information. The title of your article is "Miracle Worker Lets Friend Die."

Be sure your article:
1) Catches your readers' attention.
2) Includes all of the important facts.
3) Concludes with why you think things happened as they did.

Miracle Worker Lets Friend Die

Dear Diary

Assignment: You are Martha. Jesus has been a close friend to you, your sister Mary, and your brother Lazarus. You have been keeping a diary. Your assignment is to write about what is happening in your life. Use John 11:17-37 as your source of information. Begin today's diary with the statement; "Jesus finally arrived, four days too late."

Be sure to include in your diary the following items:
1) All of the relevant information about what is happening.
2) How you and your sister are feeling about the events.
3) What conclusions you can draw from all that has happened.

DEAR DIARY.

SPIES R US

Assignment: You are a private investigator. You were hired by the enemies of Jesus, the Pharisees. They sent you from Jerusalem. The Pharisees have received reports that Jesus has been sighted a couple of miles outside the town of Bethany. The Pharisees are worried that he might stir up more trouble for them. Jesus has been constantly undercutting their authority as religious leaders. They ask you to set up a stakeout and report back if you observe Jesus doing anything out of the ordinary. You arrive in Bethany just in time to spot Jesus approaching a tomb. Use John 11:38-46 as your source of material. Be sure to include the following in your report:

1) All of the important facts.
2) Your own reaction, as well as others' reactions to what Jesus did.
3) Your conclusions about how Jesus' activities might affect the reputation of the Pharisees.
4) What you think the Pharisees can do to keep Jesus from causing them any further problems.

From the Desk of **SPIES R US** Investigations

Jesus the Ultimate Lifesaver

1) Do you know that you have victory over death?
How do you know?

2) How can knowing that Jesus has the power to raise you up from the dead help you live your life now?

3) Do some of your friends or family need Jesus, the Ultimate Lifesaver?
____Yes ____ No

Who are they?

Name _____

Name _____

Name _____

How might you help them to meet him?

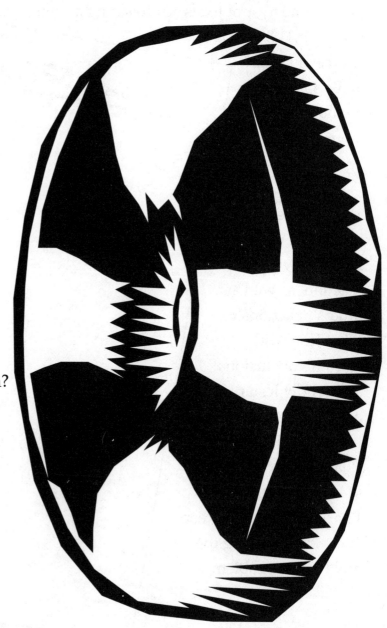

Lesson 8
Jesus Encounters Mary and Judas
Making Wise "Investments"

Overview

This lesson is designed to show students that making the decision to honor Jesus is the best investment they can ever make. Everyone decides to use their time, energy, talents, and money for something. This lesson will show that only Jesus is worthy of our devotion.

Introduction (10 minutes)

This section is designed to get your students thinking about what is important enough to spend money on.

1) Pull out your checkbook and write out a check for one million dollars. Pass the check around.

2) Ask your students to brainstorm as to what they would do with this money if the check were written out to them. Encourage everyone to come up with a suggestion. As the students mention ideas, write them on the whiteboard or easel.

3) Ask your students to vote, by raising their hands, for the top five things they would do with the money.

4) Rank the top five choices.

5) Have your students share briefly why they chose some things over others.

MATERIALS NEEDED

✔ Checkbook and pen
✔ Whiteboard or easel and markers
✔ Copy of *That's Life* (page 71)
✔ Poster board
✔ Overhead projector and transparency (optional)
✔ Wristwatch with alarm
✔ Sweat sock
✔ Four copies of *Pay Me Now or Pay Me Later* (pages 72–74)
✔ Large plastic garbage bag
✔ Balloons
✔ Marker
✔ Straight pin
✔ Copies of *Eternity Investments, Inc.* (page 75)

DIGGING IN

1) Read over the parallel account of this story found in Matthew 26:6-16. Ask, "What do you learn about the end results of Mary's actions from this passage? What do you learn about the end results of Judas' actions from this passage?"

2) The perfume that Mary poured on Jesus was probably worth about a year's wages. What do you think motivated her to pour this expensive perfume on Jesus? What do you think motivated Judas to act as he did?

3) Do you think it makes sense to invest your time, energy, talents, money and possessions in serving Jesus? Why or why not? How can knowing Jesus motivate you to serve him?

Participation (10 Minutes)

The purpose of this section is to help students see the importance of evaluating how they are investing their lives.

1) Announce that you will be playing a game similar to *Hot Potato*.

2) Copy the *That's Life* worksheet (page 71) onto a posterboard before the lesson; then place it so all your students can see it. As an option, you can make a transparency of the worksheet and put it on an overhead projector screen.

3) Give the following directions for the game:

a) The object of the game is to avoid being caught with the hot potato in your hands when the alarm sounds.

b) The person with the hot potato must read the first item on the overhead before throwing the potato to someone else.

c) Each person must read the next item on the list before throwing the hot potato to someone else. If all of the items on the list have been read before the alarm sounds, the players start over at the top of the list again.

4) Start each round by setting the alarm on your watch to go off a minute after the game begins. That way the alarm should sound anywhere from one to sixty seconds.

5) After you have set the alarm, begin the game by stuffing the watch in a sweat sock and tossing it to someone.

6) After you have played a few rounds, say something like, "For many people, their purpose in life is to accomplish all of the tasks on the list we read during this game. While there is nothing wrong with any of the items on that list, none of those things will last. This lesson focuses on investing your life in things that have eternal value. "

Observation (10 minutes)

This section lets students observe the results of investing their lives in various options.

1) Recruit four willing students to perform the skit *Pay Me Now or Pay Me Later* (pages 72–74). Give each volunteer a copy of the script to look over. Make sure they have the necessary props. [**Note:** You can perform this skit as Reader's Theater, but it will be more effective if you select your volunteers beforehand. They can practice the skit ahead of time so they feel comfortable with their lines and their characters. Also, have your actors arrange the stage area before the lesson begins.]

2) Have your volunteers introduce and perform the skit, *Pay Me Now or Pay Me Later.*

3) Before moving on, have the audience applaud and thank the performers.

Instruction (10 minutes)

This section teaches your students that using what they have to honor Jesus gives life lasting purpose and meaning.

1) Begin by saying, "The story we are about to read contrasts two people who both felt they knew which investments would give them purpose and meaning in life."

2) Ask your students to listen for similarities and differences between Mary and Judas as you read the story.

3) Read John 11:57-12:11.

4) Now write *similarities* on one side of the whiteboard and *differences* on the other side.

5) Have students call out as many similarities or differences between Judas and Mary as they can think of as you write the responses on the board.

6) Make the following brief observations:

   a) Mary understood that Jesus was worthy of her love and devotion. She gladly offered him her most valuable possession. Judas refused to fully trust Jesus. He was looking out for himself, just in case Jesus did not come through for him.

   b) For Mary, investing her life and possessions in pleasing Jesus gave her a lasting satisfaction. For Judas, investing his life and possessions in serving himself gave him only temporary satisfaction.

Application (10 minutes)

This section will help your students consider how they can wisely invest the things God has given them.

1) Pass out copies of *Eternity Investments, Inc.* (page 75).

2) Give your students five minutes to complete the worksheet.

3) When they have finished, have a few volunteers share any new "investments" in eternity they would like to start making.

4) Close in prayer, focusing on the new, eternal investments that students are now making. Be available after the meeting in case other students want to talk with you about their "investments."

THAT'S LIFE

- GO TO SCHOOL
- GET GOOD GRADES
- GO TO COLLEGE
- GET A DEGREE
- GET A GOOD JOB
- GET MARRIED
- BUY THINGS
- HAVE KIDS
- SAVE FOR YOUR KIDS SO THAT THEY CAN . . .

Pay Me Now or Pay Me Later

Characters Amy: average high school student
Lisa: airhead high school student
Salesman: slick shyster type
Re Ality: blunt practical type

Props   Two chairs
Large plastic garbage bag
Five or six inflated balloons (each balloon should have a different word written on it in marker.)
A straight pin

(Play begins with Lisa and Amy sitting around Lisa's living room with nothing to do.)

Amy: Life is such a bore. Nothing I do really means anything. I feel like a zit on the face of life.

Lisa: I know what you mean. But maybe you should try doing what I do. I'm drinking milk. My life may be a dud now, but in a few years, if I keep drinking milk, everything will be great.

Amy: *(Sarcastically)* Yeah, right.

Salesman: *(knocking at the door and carrying garbage bags filled with balloons)* Knock, knock.

Lisa: *(excited)* Get the door, Amy. Maybe it's a guy!

Amy: *(opening the door)* You rang?

Salesman: I understand your life is a drag.

Amy: Yeah, but how did you know?

Salesman: I have my ways. Now listen, I have some items in this bag that are guaranteed to give your life true purpose and meaning.

Amy: *(skeptical)* I don't think so.

Salesman: Don't be so sure. Look, here is a real hot item. I've been selling a lot of this lately. *(He pulls out a balloon with the word* boyfriend *on it.)*

Lisa: *(standing up and rushing over to the door)* Like, what is it?

Salesman: This is the promise of a boyfriend. Get one of these and your life will suddenly be worth living. Everything will fall into place once you have a boyfriend.

| Amy: | I'll take that. *(She grabs the balloon out of the salesman's hand.)* |

| Lisa: | *(disappointed)* Hey, what about me? |

| Salesman: | Relax; I've got a lot more things where that came from. Take this item for example. *(Salesman pulls another balloon out of the bag with* sports *written on it.)* |

| Lisa: | Cool. What is it? |

| Salesman: | This baby is running a real close second to boyfriends. It's called sports. If you become a jock you will never feel like you are missing out on anything again. |

| Lisa: | I'll take it. *(Lisa grabs the balloon.)* Like this is totally awesome. |

| Salesman: | Well, I've got to run. But because you're both such good customers I'll give you each a special bonus item. |

| Lisa: | Unbelievable, dude! What is it? |

| Salesman: | This is what I call the emergency happiness item. Just in case a boyfriend or sports are not enough, just pull out this beauty and bingo! All of your problems are solved. It's called things. |

| Amy: | How do you use it? |

| Salesman: | It's easy. Anytime you are bored with life, spend some money on something you really want. Go shopping, go to a movie. Spend your money on anything that will give you pleasure or keep you occupied. As a matter of fact some of my best customers depend on money and the things money can buy almost twenty-four hours a day. |

| Amy: | How much will this cost us? |

| Salesman: | Don't worry about it. All I ask is that you invest your lifetime in using my products. You can pay me in hundreds of easy installments. Just give me a week here, a day there. You'd be surprised how the hours add up. |

| Amy: | Great! We'll each take one. *(Amy and Lisa each take a balloon from the Salesman.)* |

| Salesman: | Now remember: If for some reason these items don't do the job, I've got plenty more where these came from. *(Salesman leaves)* |

| Lisa: | This is unbelievable. This guy shows up just when we need him the most. We've got some great stuff here. Like, I can't wait to start using it. |

Re Ality:	*(Re Ality comes and knocks at the door)* Knock, Knock.
Amy:	Now what? *(She goes and opens the door)*
Re Ality:	Good evening, ladies. Ality's my name, Re Ality. I hear you recently purchased some new toys to keep your lives interesting and meaningful.
Amy:	Yeah, but how did you know?
Re Ality:	I have my ways. Now let me take a look at what you've got.
Lisa:	Sure, Mr. Ality, check this out. *(Lisa holds up the balloon with* sports *written on it)* Isn't it, like, totally awesome?
Re Ality:	Sports, eh? That's nice—but what happens when you get injured or don't make the team? Or what if you win everything? What have you really got to show for it that will last? No, I'm afraid that sports just doesn't cut it. *(Re Ality pulls out a pin and pops Lisa's balloon.)*
Lisa:	*(extremely upset)* Hey, look what you did to my sports!
Re Ality:	That's life, baby.
Amy:	Well, what about this? *(She holds up her boyfriend balloon.)*
Re Ality:	Better, but it still doesn't cut it. What about the boy that dumps you or uses you? What if you finally get the hunk of your dreams and he turns out to be boring? Even if he turns out to be everything you ever wanted, he still won't be perfect. And even if he *were* perfect, why would he want to be with you when you're not perfect? No, I'm afraid this one has to go too. *(Amy tries to pull her balloon back but Re Ality pops it anyway.)*
Amy:	Hey, that really hurt! Why don't you get out of here and don't bother coming back!
Re Ality:	Don't worry, I'll be back. *(Re Ality leaves)*
Lisa:	Man, that stinks! That guy was a real loser.
Amy:	Yeah. Its a good thing he didn't see our other balloons or he would have tried to pop those too.
Lisa:	I think we need to go find the guy with all the balloons. I need something to keep me going.
Amy:	Just drink your milk, Lisa.

ETERNITY INVESTMENTS, INC.

"We take investments to a whole new level"

Investment Portfolio for _____

=============== P E R S O N A L   A S S E T S ===============

1) Talents, Abilities, and Interests

My talents, abilities, and interests include:

_____

Some ways I could to invest these assets for Jesus Christ are:

_____

2) Friendships, Relationships, and Other People

My personal relationships include the following people:

_____

Some ways I could invest my relationships with people for Jesus Christ are:

_____

3) Money, Possessions, Jobs, and Other Responsibilities

My money, possessions, jobs, and other areas of responsibility include:

_____

Some ways I could invest these assets for Jesus Christ are:

_____

"But store up for yourself treasures in heaven, where moth and rust do not destroy, and where thieves do not break in and steal. For where your treasure is, there your heart will be also" (Matthew 6:20-21).

Lesson 9
Jesus Encounters Peter
Handling Opposition
John 13:36-38; 15:18-16:4; 18:12-27

Overview
This lesson is designed to prepare your students for the reality that when they decide to follow Jesus, they will face opposition. They need to know that when they openly identify themselves as followers of Jesus, some people will view them as their enemies.

Introduction (10 minutes)
This section gets your students thinking about being prepared for opposition.

1) Ask for several volunteers to participate in a book-balancing contest.
2) Tell the volunteers that they will need to leave the room while you set up an obstacle course for them.
3) After the volunteers leave, set up chairs at the end of the room for each of them to walk around. Arm the rest of the students with water guns, pillows, paper wads, and other items to distract the volunteers and throw them off balance.
4) Instruct the students to hide their "weapons" and wait until the volunteers begin the contest before the attack. Once the contest begins, the other students should yell, scream, and use their weapons to throw the volunteers off balance. However, the group must stay several feet away from the participants, and not touch them.
5) Bring the volunteers back into the room, and give them each a book to balance on their heads. Outline the following directions:

MATERIALS NEEDED

✔ Books
✔ Water guns
✔ Pillows
✔ Paper wads
✔ Vehicles and drivers
✔ Pencils
✔ Bibles
✔ Copies of *Peter: A Case Study in Handling Opposition* (page 81)
✔ Blank postcards

1) Read over John 15:18-20. What does Jesus say is the relationship between the way the people of the world treat him and the way they will treat his followers? Why is this so?

2) If unbelievers are not treating those that believe in Jesus the same way they treated Jesus, what do you think that would mean?

3) Can you think of some natural ways you can identify yourself as a follower of Christ to those around you? What are they?

a) Start out together with the book balanced on your head.

b) At the signal, walk to the other end of the room, around the chair, and back with the book balanced on your head.

c) If the book falls off, or if anyone touches the book with his or her hands, that person is disqualified.

6) After the contest is over, ask for more volunteers to compete in the same contest. Repeat the contest, only this time, allow the volunteers to remain in the room while the audience "re-arms."

7) After the contest, gather up all of the items you distributed. Ask your students to describe the difference between the way the first group of volunteers handled the contest and the way the second group handled the contest. Point out that expecting opposition can help us be prepared to stand up against attacks.

Participation (20–30 minutes)

This section uses a simulation experience to help students feel what it's like to face opposition for being Christians.

1) Tell your students that they are going on a short field trip. Do not tell them where you are going. [**Note:** You may need to recruit parents or other adults to aid with transportation.]

2) Load the entire group into vehicles and take them to a mall, bowling alley, or some other nearby popular hangout where they are sure to run into kids they know.

3) When the kids arrive at their destination, have them form groups of three or four students each.

4) Give one person in each group a pencil and the work sheet *Peter: A Case Study in Handling Opposition* (page 81). Also, give Bibles to every group member.

5) Tell your students that you want each group to go to different spots on the premises and complete the worksheet together. Give them ten minutes to complete the worksheet, then return to the vehicles. You will probably encounter a wide range of reactions from your students when you give this assignment. Expect some

negative or fearful reactions, or some expressions of reticence. These feelings will help drive home the point of the assignment later in the lesson.

Observation (10 minutes)

This section provides a debriefing time. Your students will have a chance to identify some of their negative feelings when they encounter opposition for being identified with Jesus.

1) After you return from the field trip, ask one person from each group to share his or her answers from the worksheet. (Your students may have a variety of answers to this worksheet. The point is to help your students put themselves in Peter's shoes and identify with how he may have felt.)

2) Ask your students what they thought others around them were thinking about them as they worked on the Bible lesson.

3) Ask what thoughts and feelings they experienced that might have been similar to how Peter may have felt.

4) Continue the discussion by having students share why it may feel uncomfortable to be be identified as followers of Christ. In addition to the students' answers, you can suggest that unbelievers may view Christians as snobs, gullible, self-righteous, flakes, or fanatics.

Instruction (5 minutes)

This section is designed to teach your students that encountering opposition is a natural part of following Christ. They do not need to be surprised or discouraged by it.

1) Say something like, "Peter felt he would never be overcome by opposition when he promised Jesus that he would follow him anywhere. I want to read you the preparation speech Jesus gave Peter and the rest of the disciples. I think you will find that most of it can also apply to you. "

2) Read John 15:18-16:4, then state the following observations from the passage:

    a) Anytime you identify yourself publicly with Jesus you become a natural enemy to the general population. You can expect this to happen.

    b) By identifying yourself publicly with Jesus, you are admitting you need him to forgive you of your sins. Many people don't like to think about this because it reminds them of their own sin.

c) Jesus gave a warning so that his followers would not be discouraged or shocked when people opposed them. Opposition is a sign that you are following Jesus.

Application (5 minutes)
This section challenges your students to look for opportunities to identify themselves with Jesus, and it provides encouragement for those students who are ready to make this commitment.

1) Pass out a blank postcard and pencil to each student.
2) Ask them to think about whether they are willing to identify themselves as followers of Christ whenever they have the opportunity.
3) Tell them that if they decide they want to make that commitment, they should write their name and address on the postcard so that you can send them a note of encouragement and pray for them later in the week.
4) Collect all of the cards and pencils. Be sure to send a brief message of encouragement to those that addressed the postcards later in the week.

Peter: A Case Study in Handling Opposition

Read John 13:36-38.

1) What was Peter's attitude at this time?

2) If you could have taken Peter aside and given him a little advice, what would you have said to him?

Read John 18:12-27.

1) What were Peter's attitudes and feelings at this time?

2) Do you think Peter was really expecting this kind of opposition when he promised to follow Jesus? Why or why not?

3) Peter seemed to completely change his attitude about being identified with Jesus. What do you think caused this change of heart?

Lesson 10

Jesus Encounters His Disciples #1
Producing Fruit in Our Lives

John 15:5-17

Overview

This lesson is designed to teach your students what it means to remain connected to Jesus so that he can produce godly characteristics in their lives.

Introduction (20 minutes)

This section introduces the lesson by having your students play a game involving various kinds of fruit.

1) You will need to prepare before class by completing the following tasks:

    a) Estimate the number of teams you will have if you divide your students into groups of three to five people each.

    b) For each team, place in a grocery bag an apple, an orange, a lemon, a banana, and a small cluster of grapes.

    c) Make enough copies of *Fruit Relay* (page 87) for each team to have a set of instructions. Cut the instructions into five separate pieces of paper, fold them over and place them in separate plastic buckets (or other containers) for each team.

2) Tell your students that they will be running a relay. Have your students form teams of five, if possible. If there are less than five people on a team, some players can go twice.

3) Ask each team to line up. Across the room from each team, place a

MATERIALS NEEDED

✔ Grocery bags

✔ Apples, oranges, lemons, bananas, and grapes

✔ Plastic buckets or other containers

✔ Pencils

✔ Copies of *Fruit Relay* (page 87)

✔ A deck of playing cards

✔ Copies of *The Flavor of Fruit* (page 89)

✔ Copies of *The Power Source* table tent (page 90)

1) **Read John 15:9-11 again. What do these verses say about remaining in the middle of Christ's love? What does Jesus promise those who obey him?**

2) **Do you think it is possible for a person to have the strength to obey Christ's commands? How? (Hint: see verse 5.)**

3) **Have you ever felt that it was too hard to please God? Why or why not? Are there areas in your life where you have failed God time and time again? How can the illustration Jesus gave about the vine and the branches help you approach pleasing God differently?**

grocery bag with the fruit in it next to a plastic bucket or other container with the instructions in it.

4) Explain the relay as follows:

    a) At *go*, the first person on each team runs to his or her container, picks up one of the pieces of paper, reads it, and does what it says.

    b) After each task is completed, the next player follows the same procedure.

    c) The team to complete all five tasks first is the winner.

5) When the game is over, tell your students that Jesus compared a successful life to a tree that bears fruit. Ask them to share why they think "fruit" is a good symbol of success for followers of Jesus.

Participation (10 minutes)

This section helps your students think about how important it is to be attentive and connected to their leaders if they are going to accomplish their goals.

1) Have your students form two teams. Have team members hold hands and sit face-to-face with the opposite team.

2) The leader or an extra player should sit at on one end of the rows and hold hands with of the end player on each team. Place a piece of fruit at the other end of the two rows.

3) When the leader is ready, he or she squeezes both end players' hands. They in turn squeeze the hand of the persons next to them.

4) When the last person on each team has had his or her hand squeezed, this person should pick up the piece of fruit at the end of the row with his or her free hand. The team that picks up the fruit first wins.

5) Play this game several times, allowing various students to be the leader.

Instruction (10 minutes)

This section shows your students that they cannot demonstrate godly characteristics unless they stay in contact with Jesus.

1) Start by saying, "In the game we just played, it was important to stay connected to the leader and be ready to respond to his or her actions. In the Scripture passage we are about to read, Jesus talks about how important it is to stay connected to him if we are going to have a fruitful Christian life."

2) Read John 15:5-17. Make the following brief observations:

a) God wants to produce good fruit like love, joy, and peace in our lives.

b) Like the branches on a tree, we do not have any power to produce godly characteristics by ourselves.

c) As long as we stay connected to Jesus, God guarantees that he will produce fruit in our lives.

Observation (10 minutes)

1) Tell your students that you are going to give an amazing demonstration to illustrate what Jesus meant by remaining connected to him. (See *The Connection* on page 88 for instructions on this demonstration.)

2) Lay out nine playing cards on the floor or a table. "Choose" a so-called "volunteer". Now tell your students that you are going to leave the room while they choose a card. You will have such a good connection to your partner that you will be able to point out the card your students chose when you return.

3) Leave the room, and return when students have chosen a card. After grandstanding about how much you have to concentrate on the message your partner is sending, point out the correct card. Repeat this demonstration several times, allowing your students to guess how you were able to choose the right card every time.

4) When you have finished your demonstration, make the following observations:

a) You could not succeed without depending on your partner. Connecting with Jesus requires constantly depending on him.

b) You had to be aware of the messages your partner was sending and be ready to respond to them. Connecting with Jesus means that we are willing to listen and respond to what he says.

Application (10 minutes)

This section helps your students to think about whether God is producing fruit in their lives. It will give students a tool to remind them of their need to remain connected to Jesus.

1) Pass out copies of *The Flavor of Fruit* (page 89). Have your students read it over and write down their responses.

2) Have a few willing students share why they would like to see specific fruit produced in their lives.

3) Pass out *The Power Source* table tent (page 90) to each student. [**Note:** You may want to photocopy this onto card-stock paper.] Tell students to fold their work sheets so that a verse is on each side, and then to stand their table tents on a table or desk near their beds. Ask them to read John 15:5 just before they turn out their lights at night as a reminder that, without Jesus, they are powerless to produce fruit. Ask them to read Philippians 4:13 when they turn their lights on in the morning as a reminder that Jesus is their power source.

Fruit
Relay

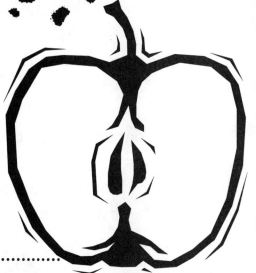

Pick up the apple, bring it back to your team. Hold the apple by the stem while two of your team members eat it until only the core remains. Return the core to the fruit bag.

Pick up the orange, bring it back to your team. Have team members pass it chin–to–chin down the line. When the orange is passed back to you, peel it and have your team members help you eat it. Return the orange peels to the fruit bag.

Pick up the lemon. Bring it back to your team. Peel it. Have each member take turns eating a slice, while smiling, until it is gone. Return the peels to the fruit bag.

Pick up the banana. Bring it back to your team. Partially peel it. Hold it while team members take turns taking bites until it is gone. Return the peel to the fruit bag.

Pick up the cluster of grapes. Bring it back to your team. Give each person a grape. Ask team members to take turns lobbing a grape into another team member's mouth. When each team member has successfully caught a grape in his or her mouth, bring the remaining grapes back and put it in the fruit bag.

The Connection

1) Recruit a student to be your "volunteer" before class.

2) The trick is:

a) Lay out three rows of cards with three cards in each row.

b) Have your "volunteer" sit facing the cards with his or her legs visible to you.

c) Your "volunteer" indicates to you which card was chosen by where he or she places his or her hand on his or her leg.

THE FLAVOR OF FRUIT

If you could cut open a piece of "spiritual fruit," some of its flavors would include:

__Love
__Joy
__Peace
__Patience
__Kindness
__Goodness
__Faithfulness
__Gentleness
__Self–control

Put a check by the flavors you think you needed the most in your life lately. Why did you check the flavors you did?

This week's assignment: Concentrate on staying connected with Jesus this week. Keep a short daily journal, and record any fruit you observe Jesus beginning to produce in your life. Be sure to indicate how *you* can tell the fruit is emerging.

Day 1	Day 2	Day 3	Day 4	Day 5	Day 6	Day 7

Galatians 5:22-23 "But the fruit of the Spirit is love, joy, peace, patience, kindness, goodness, faithfulness, gentleness and self–control. Against such things there is no law."

The Power Source

The Power Source

The Power Source

Philippians 4:13
"I can do all things through him who gives me strength."

The Power Source

Philippians 4:13
"I can do all things through him who gives me strength."

The Power Source

Philippians 4:13
"I can do all things through him who gives me strength."

The Power Source

The Power Source

John 15:5
"I am the vine; you are the branches. If a man remains in me and I in him, he will bear much fruit; apart from me you can do nothing."

The Power Source

John 15:5
"I am the vine; you are the branches. If a man remains in me and I in him, he will bear much fruit; apart from me you can do nothing."

The Power Source

John 15:5
"I am the vine; you are the branches. If a man remains in me and I in him, he will bear much fruit; apart from me you can do nothing."

Lesson 11
Jesus Encounters His Disciples #2
Recognizing the Holy Spirit

John 14:15-27; 16:5-16

Overview

This lesson is designed to help your students realize that the Holy Spirit is God. They will learn that he is a person and that he lives inside each believer. Students will realize that he wants to have an active and vital relationship with them. This lesson will also help your students to understand that God has given each of them the Holy Spirit as a personal guide and source of power.

Introduction (10 minutes)

This section starts your students thinking about the Holy Spirit.

1) Ask your students to call out the first thing that comes to mind when they hear the word *spirit*. Next have them call out the first thing that comes to mind when they hear *Holy Spirit*. (The purpose of this exercise is to help your students verbalize any thoughts they might have about the identity of the Holy Spirit. You're not necessarily looking for right or wrong answers).

2) Show the clip from *Angels in the Outfield* (available in most video stores) where Al (the head angel) first comes to visit the little boy, Roger, at the baseball stadium. (If you are unable to find this video, have your students describe various ghosts, angels, or spirits they have seen in movies.)

3) After watching the clip, have your students describe ways they think the Holy Spirit might be similar to the angel in this scene. Then have them describe what ways they think the Holy Spirit might be different

MATERIALS NEEDED

✔ Copy of the video *Angels in the Outfield*

✔ TV

✔ VCR

✔ Tape

✔ Drawing paper or white construction paper

✔ Crayons or markers

✔ Copy of *You Can Be the Artist!* (page 95)

✔ Copy of *You Can Be the Artist Again!* (page 96)

✔ Whiteboard or easel with markers

✔ Copies of *Spirit Simile* (page 97)

✔ Pencils

DIGGING IN

1) Carefully read over John 14:16-27. These verses talk about the Father, the Son, and the Holy Spirit. According to this passage, how do they relate to each other?

2) Jesus promises that the Holy Spirit (the Comforter) will live in believers. When the Spirit is living in you, who else does this passage say lives in you?

3) What differences would you expect to see in someone if God was living in them?

from this angel. (Again, the purpose for asking these questions is to start your students thinking about who the Holy Spirit is and what he is like.)

Observation (15 minutes)

This section shows your students the advantage of having someone to act as a personal tutor.

1) Before the lesson begins, tape four pieces of paper (approximately 2' x 2' square) to a wall.

2) Ask for three volunteers. Give two of the volunteers markers or crayons. Give the third volunteer a copy of the drawing on *You Can Be an Artist!* (page 95). Do not show this drawing to the other two "artists."

3) Give the volunteers the following instructions:

a) The "artists" are to each choose one of the papers taped to the wall. As the third student describes a drawing to them, the artists are to try to duplicate it on the paper.

b) The student describing the drawing is to stand with his or her back to the artists as he or she describes the drawing.

c) The artists are not allowed to look at the original drawing or ask any questions of their "tutor."

4) After the artists are done, compare their drawings to see how close they came to duplicating the original.

5) Now have the artists try the same exercise with the drawing found on *You Can Be an Artist Again!* (page 96). This time the tutor can face the artists so that he or she can see what they are drawing. The artists may also ask questions to help clarify what the tutor is saying.

6) When the artists are done, display the drawings to see how close they came to the original. (If all goes well, the second set of drawings will be much closer to the original than the first!)

7) Have your students discuss why the second set of drawings

were closer to the original than the first set. Be sure to point out that it is much easier to follow instructions when someone is personally guiding and interacting with you than when you are simply receiving abstract instructions.

Instruction (15 minutes)

This section provides an opportunity for students to investigate what the Scriptures say about the Holy Spirit.

1) Start out by saying, "When Jesus was ready to return to his Father in heaven, his disciples were feeling abandoned. Jesus wanted his followers to know that he was not deserting them, instead the Holy Spirit would be coming to be with them forever."

2) Tell your students you are going to read what Jesus said to his disciples. Ask them to interrupt you any time they hear information about the Holy Spirit.

3) Read John 14:15-27 and John 16:5-16. As the interruptions come, have a student volunteer write the information shared about the Holy Spirit on the whiteboard or easel.

4) When you've finished reading, have one of your students read the information about the Holy Spirit from the whiteboard or easel. Emphasize the following observations about the Holy Spirit from the Scripture passage:

a) The Holy Spirit is the personal guide and counselor for all believers because he actually lives in them.

b) The followers of Jesus can depend on the Holy Spirit to help them understand what God is saying to them.

c) You are not alone when you attempt to bring Christ to unbelievers. The Holy Spirit is working to convince people of their need for God.

Participation (10 minutes)

This section helps your students picture the Holy Spirit's role in their lives.

1) Pass out copies of *Spirit Simile* (page 97).

2) Read the directions aloud, then allow your students a few minutes to complete their descriptions.

3) When your students have finished, have a few willing volunteers share what they wrote.

Application (5 minutes)

This section is designed to help your students to become more aware of the presence of the Holy Spirit in their lives.

1) Write the equation $a+b=x$ on the whiteboard or easel.

2) Then say, "If a = you and b = the Holy Spirit, what kinds of things would you expect to happen if b were added to a?" You may want to share ways that you have seen evidence of the Holy Spirit's presence in your own life to get the discussion started. Have your students share their ideas. Add some of the following ideas if your students have not mentioned them:

   a. A desire to know God and understand his Word.

   b. A desire and power to change wrong attitudes and actions.

   c. The desire and strength to serve others and introduce people to Christ.

   d. The ability to persevere through adverse circumstances.

3) Tell your students that you are assigning them to be on a "Spirit Watch." Ask them to act as detectives over the next week. Tell them to keep a journal of any actions, feelings, or experiences that they have during the week that might show the Holy Spirit's presence in their lives.

4) Be sure to check back with students at the beginning of next week's meeting to see what they discovered about the Holy Spirit.

YOU CAN BE AN ARTIST!

YOU CAN BE AN ARTIST AGAIN!

Spirit Simile

When you create a mental picture of something, it can seem more real. Take a moment to imagine what the Holy Spirit is like and how he relates to you.

Here is an example:

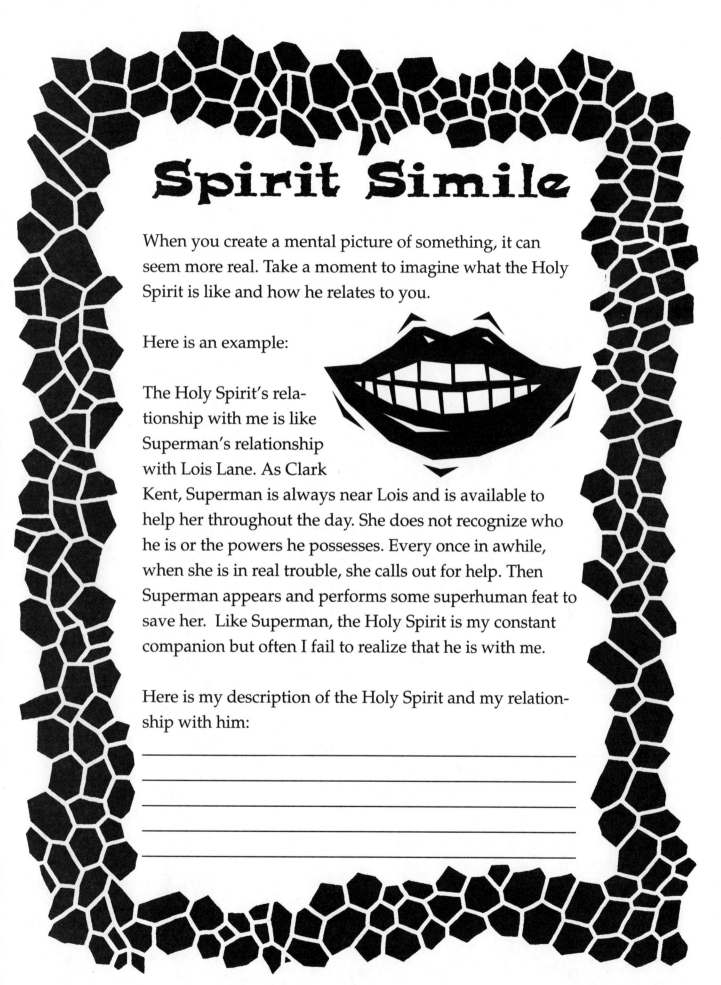

The Holy Spirit's relationship with me is like Superman's relationship with Lois Lane. As Clark Kent, Superman is always near Lois and is available to help her throughout the day. She does not recognize who he is or the powers he possesses. Every once in awhile, when she is in real trouble, she calls out for help. Then Superman appears and performs some superhuman feat to save her. Like Superman, the Holy Spirit is my constant companion but often I fail to realize that he is with me.

Here is my description of the Holy Spirit and my relationship with him:

_____

_____

_____

_____

_____

Lesson
Jesus Encounters Mary Magdalene
Believing the Impossible

12

John 19:23-25; 20:1-3, 10-18

Overview

This lesson is designed to give your students confidence that the resurrection of Jesus Christ is both an historically credible event and convincing proof of his divine power.

Introduction (10 minutes)

This section starts your students thinking about individuals who have made great comebacks by overcoming seemingly impossible odds.

1) Tell your students that you are going to read five accounts of individuals who have made great comebacks. Then, read the stories from *Amazing Comebacks* (page 103). After you read each story, have a student put the individual's name on the whiteboard or easel.

2) After you have read all five stories, have your students vote, with a show of hands, on which comeback they thought was the most amazing. Record the number of votes beside each name on your whiteboard or easel.

3) Allow students to share other amazing comebacks they know of.

Participation (15 minutes)

This section uses an entertaining activity to demonstrate the reality of the Resurrection.

1) Introduce the melodrama *The Great Resurrection Debate* by saying

MATERIALS NEEDED

✔ Copy of *Amazing Comebacks* (page 103)
✔ Whiteboard or easel and markers
✔ Copy of *The Great Resurrection Debate* (page 104–106)
✔ Tape player
✔ Cassette tape of the song *Sunday's On the Way* from the album *The Absolute Best* by Carmen (optional)
✔ Copies of *If Easter Never Happened* (page 107)
✔ Pencils
✔ Chips and dip
✔ Punch or soda
✔ Paper plates and napkins
✔ Paper cups

DIGGING IN

1) Read John 19:23-25; 20: 1-3; and 20:10-18 again. What do you notice about where Mary is and what she is doing in each of these passages? (You may need to point out to your students that she is always where she expects Jesus to be. She is always wanting to be in his presence. Even after he is dead, she is longing for his presence.)

2) Jesus went out of his way to appear to Mary before he returned to his Father. Why do you think Jesus chose to appear to Mary before anyone else, including his closest friends, the disciples?

3) If you related to Jesus more as Mary Magdalene did, what would you do differently?

something like, "Undoubtedly, the most amazing comeback ever was when Jesus came back from the dead. Because this event was so extraordinary, some people question whether the Resurrection really took place."

2) Announce to your students that they are about to perform a melodrama entitled *The Great Resurrection Debate.*

3) Assign uninhibited volunteers to play the various roles in the melodrama. Let the audience know that they are part of the melodrama—it is important for them to actively respond to the words of the narrator.

4) You will be the narrator. As with any melodrama, the part of the narrator is crucial.

> a) The narrator must be ready to pause frequently so that the people acting and the audience can respond to what is being said. This ability to interact will add to the humor and effectiveness of this melodrama.
>
> b) Be sure to read through the script ahead of time so you can picture how the melodrama is supposed to work and where it is headed.
>
> c) Arrange the characters in their proper places before the melodrama begins.

4) When everyone is in place, perform the melodrama. [**Note:** This drama requires no preparation by the characters and no props.]

5) When the melodrama has finished, thank all of the participants before moving on.

Instruction (10 minutes)

This section uses the story of Mary Magdalene to demonstrate the transforming power that the resurrection of Jesus Christ can have on those who believe.

1) Recruit three volunteers to each read one of the following three passages: John 19:23-25; John 20:1-3; John 20:10-18. After

each passage is read, pause and invite a willing student to summarize what happened and how Mary Magdalene was involved.

2) Ask your students what emotions they think Mary may have felt during these events. Be sure they notice the following emotions: horror, despair, grief, hopelessness, surprise, disbelief, shock, joy, and hope.

3) Briefly make the following observations from the passages:

a) The resurrection of Jesus Christ overshadowed all of the sad circumstances that preceded it. He immediately gave Mary joy.

b) The resurrection demonstrated victory over the most impossible situation. When Mary realized Jesus had overcome death, her hope was renewed.

c) The resurrection of Jesus Christ can be life-changing news to anyone willing to accept it. Mary went on to spread the news that Jesus was alive.

Observation (10 minutes)

This section demonstrates to your students the difference the resurrection of Jesus makes on the world.

1) Pass out copies of *If Easter Had Never Happened* (page 107). Have your students fill it out.

2) When your students have finished, ask a few volunteers share some of the things they wrote. If your students don't mention them, you may want to add the following observations:

a) The world would be ruled by Satan. The terrible and painful effects of sin would go unchecked.

b) There would be no prospect of justice or peace for the future.

c) People would be forced to serve Satan, who does not care about them or want what is best for them.

 Option

Introduce the song *Sunday's on the Way* by saying, "This song tells how the resurrection might have affected Satan and what the Resurrection can mean to you." Play the song for your students.

Application (5 minutes)

This section provides your students with an opportunity to celebrate what the resurrection of Jesus Christ means to them personally.

1) Serve chips, dip, and punch or soda.
2) Ask your students to let the chips and dip serve as a reminder that Jesus not only went down into the grave but came back out victorious.
3) As they eat, encourage students to share with someone around them how the resurrection of Jesus Christ has changed their lives.

Amazing Comebacks

Harry Houdini

Harry Houdini had a reputation as a master magician. He was especially well known for his ability as an escape artist. Frequently, Houdini would challenge people to try to confine him in such a way that he could not escape. On one occasion, he allowed himself to be shackled and placed in a box which was then locked and tied shut with rope. The box was then submerged underwater. As usual, Houdini escaped unharmed.

Angela Bondini

Angela Bondini staged an amazing comeback when she returned to the surface of the water, after plunging to a depth of 351 feet while holding her breath. She remained underwater for a total of two minutes and forty-one seconds.*

George Foreman

George Foreman became the heavyweight boxing champion of the world at age 25 by defeating Joe Frazier. He lost his title shortly thereafter to Muhammed Ali. Many boxing fans felt Foreman was foolish when he decided to attempt a comeback twenty years later. But at the age of 45, George Foreman shocked the sports world by knocking out the reigning champion. He became the oldest heavyweight champion in the history of boxing.

Sauer

A Doberman pinscher named of Sauer demonstrated an incredible ability to bring back a criminal. This dog tracked down a thief for 100 miles by scent alone.*

Frank Reich

On June 3, 1993, Frank Reich found himself in an impossible situation. He was the backup quarterback for the Buffalo Bills. Because starter Jim Kelly was injured, Reich was called to start against the Houston Oilers. By the second half, the Bills were being trounced by the Oilers by a score of 35-3. It appeared to be a hopeless situation. No team in the history of the NFL had ever come back from such a huge deficit. But on this particular occasion, Frank Reich was not to be denied. He led his team to score 35 unanswered points. They ultimately won the game in overtime.*

*The Guiness Book of World Records 1995, Guinness Publishing Ltd., 1994.

The Great Resurrection Debate

A Melodrama

Characters

> Mary Magnolia
> Martha Busybody
> The Rolling Lawn
> Thomas Doubterson
> Peter Piper
> A Sigh
> The Crowd

(The Rolling Lawn should be seated in the middle of the room with The Crowd seated around it.)

One sunny afternoon, a Crowd of students was sitting beside the Rolling Lawn outside their school building. As they sat there, they watched Mary Magnolia and her friend Martha Busybody walking along until they bumped into a classmate, Thomas Doubterson, who was walking across the Rolling Lawn after history class. The Rolling Lawn looked so pleasant as it rolled along. Mary decided to sit down on it. Martha stood silently by.

As Mary sat on the Rolling Lawn, Thomas began a discussion about the subject of their history class. He said, "Mary." Mary gave A Sigh to Thomas and said, "Yes, Thomas?" Thomas gave A Sigh back to Mary and said, "Do you really believe that Jesus rose from the dead?" Mary got off the Rolling Lawn and became quite perplexed. She paced around the Lawn several times and finally said, "Of course, Thomas. Don't you?" Thomas wrinkled his nose and said, "No."

The Crowd murmured in disbelief. They continued murmuring until Thomas finally interrupted. "It's a lie!" he shouted at the top of his lungs. Then he said softly, "I think his disciples made the whole thing up." The Crowd whispered "good point" as they tilted their heads to hear how Mary would respond. Martha stood silently by. Mary did not know how to respond. She gave A Sigh to Thomas. Thomas slowly gave A Sigh back to Mary.

Mary's friend Peter Piper, who had been standing close by, came bouncing up to them and put his foot on the Rolling Lawn (that wasn't rolling now, but had started to stand up since no one was sitting on it). Peter responded to Thomas's comment by jumping up and down while he said, "Would you die for a lie?" The Crowd loudly echoed his last words, "Die for a lie." Thomas repeated Peter's words with a puzzled look on his face, "Die for a lie?" The Crowd echoed Peter's words, "Die for a lie." Peter took his foot off the Rolling Lawn, which was starting to lean way over and wilt. He explained, "The disciples were persecuted for saying that Jesus rose from the dead." Then he said, "Surely they would not die for a lie?" The Crowd started to echo "Die for a lie" but instead they rose to their feet and yelled out in unison, "Good point, Peter!"

The Crowd dropped back down to their seats. Peter smiled at them and said "Thank you" as he wiped off his feet on the Rolling Lawn. The crowd responded in unison saying, "You're welcome, Peter."

Peter, Mary and Thomas all sat down on the Rolling Lawn as they held on to A Sigh that was struggling to get free. Finally, they let it go. Thomas stood up and looked at Mary. Martha stood silently by. Mary stood up and looked at Peter. Peter stood up and looked at The Crowd. Finally, Thomas got a funny look on his face. Thomas said, "Maybe the disciples stole the body." The Crowd turned to one another and said, "Could this be?" Peter and Mary winked at each other and said, "No way" in unison. Thomas scratched his head. He asked, "Why?" as he watched the Rolling Lawn move up and down in the wind.

Mary replied, "There were sixteen Roman soldiers guarding the tomb." Some of the Crowd said, "Wow!" while others exclaimed, "Unbelievable, dude!" The Crowd became completely quiet because they sensed that Peter was about to make an excellent point. Peter pointed his index finger right in Thomas's face and added, "Besides, the stone in front of the tomb weighed a couple of tons."

Thomas pushed Peter's hand out of his face. Peter and Thomas started pushing each other while Mary nervously picked at the Rolling Lawn. Martha stood silently by. Finally, Martha opened her mouth to speak. Peter, Thomas, and Mary turned their heads toward her and put their hands behind their ears to make sure they could hear what Martha was about to say. For ten long seconds, The Crowd broke into a cheer to encourage Martha to speak. The Crowd chanted excitedly, "Go Martha! Go Martha! Go Martha!" Peter counted to ten slowly as The Crowd chanted.

Martha finally said, in a cute little Minnie Mouse-type voice, "There were so few people that saw Jesus alive, maybe they made a mistake." Mary started to giggle and continued to giggle. Peter broke into uncontrollable laughter and continued to laugh. Even Thomas began to chuckle and continued to chuckle. The Crowd, growing impatient, put their index fingers in front of their mouths and whispered, "Sh-h-h." Peter stopped laughing. Then Mary stopped giggling. Finally, Thomas stopped chuckling.

Mary responded to her friend by saying, "There were over five hundred people who saw Jesus after he rose from the dead." Then Mary added, "And most of them knew him really well." The Crowd smiled and nodded at each other approvingly because they knew Mary had made an excellent point. Martha gave A Sigh to Mary. Mary did not accept it. She let it drop onto the Rolling Lawn. The Rolling Lawn rolled away from A Sigh. A Sigh sat sighing sadly by itself.

Martha and Thomas got into a huddle to try come up with one last reason why Jesus could not have risen from the dead. The Crowd played patty cake with each other to pass the time while Martha and Thomas consulted. Suddenly Thomas and Martha put their hands together in the middle of their huddle and yelled out, "Go team!" They then ran over and stood face-to-face with Mary and Peter.

Thomas and Martha began skipping in a circle around Mary and Peter and chanting over and over again, "Jesus never really died, he just fainted, na na na na na na." Soon The Crowd began to join in taunting Peter and Mary by saying "Jesus never really died, he just fainted, na na na na na na." Louder and louder, they chanted. Suddenly everyone became quiet. Peter raised his hand. Mary held her nose and said, "Put it down, please." The Crowd groaned. Mary finally replied to Martha after she smiled down at the Rolling Lawn and breathed A Sigh. "Martha," she said. The Crowd nudged each other and listened intently because they knew this was the closing line and it would probably be important. "Martha," she said. Martha stood silently by. "Martha," she said. Peter and Thomas perked up their ears because they knew this was the serious part of the play. "Martha," she said, and then she continued, " Witnesses saw water and blood flow from Jesus' side." Mary paused a moment to make sure everyone was listening. Then she went on to say, "His heart had completely stopped—and yet three days later, he was alive and well." Peter, Martha and Thomas all exclaimed together, "Now *that's* a miracle!" The Crowd cheered and applauded wildly.

Information concerning the resurrection taken from *A Ready Defense* by Josh McDowell; Here's Life Publishers, San Bernadino, 1990.

If Easter Never Happened

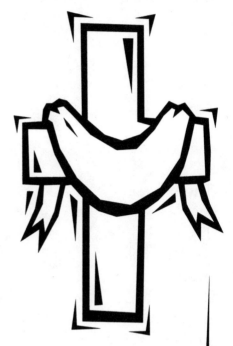

List five things that would be different in the world if Jesus had never risen from the dead:

1)

2)

3)

4)

5)

List five ways your life would be different if Jesus had never risen from the dead:

1)

2)

3)

4)

5)